D1134577

BGOL

All Things Remembered

ALL THINGS REMEMBERED

Goldie

with Ben Thompson

FABER & FABER

This edition first published in 2017
in the UK by Faber & Faber Ltd,
Bloomsbury House,
74–77 Great Russell Street,
London WC1B 3DA

Printed in the UK by CPI Group (UK) Ltd, Croydon CR0 4YY

A CIP record for this book is available from the British Library

ISBN 978–0–571–33207–6

10 9 8 7 6 5 4 3 2 1

For Marcus Kaye
39

CONTENTS

Contents / Track-Listing

Side G

Side H

Plates

Introduction

So why *All Things Remembered*? Because all these memories get put away into the deep, deep storage areas of the brain. They're not corrupt files; they're in there somewhere, we just don't access them. Until something childlike or traumatic happens, or we're brought together by loss, or laughter, or music – and that brings them all flooding back.

Then you get this fucking mad déjà vu. When that moment comes I'm like, 'Fuck, this is part of my life, I actually remember it! I've been here before.' Shit, what do you call the feeling of that sudden glimpse? Is it Proustian? When something reminds me of the smell of my first cigarette, or my fucking first smell of pussy – which tasted better by the way . . .

I think the first memory I have is of being in the womb. That's why what is called the rabbit position in yoga – where you wrap yourself up in a ball, like a foetus – is very difficult for me. Because the stress of that *in utero* situation was translated through my shoulders and my hips to such an extent that it still becomes physically apparent fifty-two years later. I one hundred per cent believe that my subconscious knew even then that me being born was going to be a problem – because my mum had a difficult pregnancy, and she had these two black guys fighting over her all the time. It caused her a lot of antenatal misery. It turns out that my subconscious was right.

One of the ways I've found of dealing with the chaos that followed is by getting in my time machine and fucking off. Not in real life – I'm not Dr Who – but in my head, which is the same thing, really. That's what my first album, *Timeless*, was all about.

The secret of time travel is that time aligns vertically, not horizontally – Sun Ra knew that, Philip K. Dick knew that, and I fucking know it – so you've got to stop worrying about moving back or forward and learn to punch through up and down.

I wanted to make this book reflect that, which is why instead of a traditional linear timeline – birth/school/work/death – it's a big stack of simultaneous past and present tenses, like the planes waiting to land at Heathrow, or a cross-section through an ants' nest. There's bound to be the odd crash, and a few poor fuckers are going to get eaten, but that's life, isn't it? No one said it was going to be easy.

When I began dredging up these memories I was halfway through making my album *The Journey Man*. At first I was very conscious of needing to keep the two things separate. After all, a book and an album are two very different things. Except as time went on I realised they're kind of not – both of them are ways of telling the story of my existence, and in the end whether the medium is recorded sound or words on a page doesn't really make much difference. Because my life's a fucking album – a really, really tumultuous long-player, with all those curves and that shimmering movement.

The vinyl edition of my difficult second album *Saturnz Return* came out across four discs – sides A–H – and a record of my life would have to be at least a quadruple fucking LP, because so much shit has happened, so that's what this one's going to be, too. There are fifty-one chapters – one for each completed year of my life – with an afterword to cover the year that's still underway at the time of writing but will be done by the time anyone's reading it. If you're a slow reader – maybe 'cos you're dyslexic like I am – you can read one chapter a week for a whole year and think of this as your Goldie almanac.

Either way, bringing together all the different narrative strands at the end was very like sequencing an album: you've got to get the right mix of ballads and bangers, happy and sad, long tracks and short ones. Hopefully I've got the EQ pretty much spot on, but only the reader can be the judge of that. See you on the other side . . .

SIDE A

When I was at the Lew Joseph children's home – on Stroud Avenue in Willenhall, in the West Midlands – there was this couple who worked there who we called Uncle Chris and Auntie Steph. They were definitely at the more laidback, trendy end of the staff in that place. They were the ones who took us to Derbyshire camping, in a minibus.

I'd been to Barmouth before, with the school, and I'd been to (I think it was) Llandudno in Wales, once, but this was a great trip. It was only going to Derbyshire, but it was amazing, because on the way there Chris introduced us to The Beatles on his eight-track in the van – *A Hard Day's Night, Revolver,* all these albums, but *Sergeant Pepper's* was the one that really stood out for me. It changed my life, really, that record. Even when I think about it now, it's still a part of me – 'When I get older, losing my hair.' When I'm sixty-four? Well, I'm only fucking thirteen years off that now! Of course sixty-four then was like a million miles away – it was like it was never going to come.

The memories I have from that trip are so beautiful to me. I just felt so good, driving through all these places in the country, and the smell of these wet fields and cow pats, and camping in a tent, with all these kids – having these sleeping bags, and the morning dew, how cold it was on your face, and how warm your body was in its little pod, and coming out into this fresh country air. It was just an amazing, amazing thing. Beans for breakfast, and bacon that was cooked outside on a stove, it felt primal; it felt like I was a caveman of some sort, on this adventure – finally living the Huckleberry Finn life; almost, I don't know. It was just a beautiful time, but what I find even more beautiful is the way the music I heard on that trip stayed with me on the journey that came after. Because of how it's tied to the memory of a certain place, a certain time, it'll always remind you of that, so you can always go back there in moments of madness.

One particular track on *Sergeant Pepper's*, the last song, 'A Day in the Life', was just unbelievable. I suppose the bit where the orchestra goes mental was one of the moments where the love of strings came into my life. And 'Lucy in the Sky with Diamonds' was just so out there in this other world. Did I really know it was based on hallucinogens? I suppose I'd heard different stories and things that were told to me, and Chris was a bit of a hippy, anyway. He'd always wear these ripped jeans – Levi's that had loads of holes with patches on them.

Weirdly enough, that's something that's always stuck with me – even now, when I go into Diesel. Renzo Rosso – the Italian guy who started that company, and still owns it outright – he's a lovely man and a really good friend of mine. I met Renzo in Miami and I stayed at his place when me and Björk had our crazy break-up. We were going to get engaged, we were going to get this house, we were going to get married, but then some personal stuff happened and it just didn't work out. It wasn't the right time, and we split up. But it kind of devastated me a bit, to be honest.

Anyway, the whole thing that was funny with Renzo and his Diesel jeans was that I'd always put holes in my jeans and have patches on them, just purely because of the memory of Chris and his jeans, how cool I thought they looked. Of course, looking back thirty-five or forty years after that event, you know that those jeans were only scrap jeans that you'd throw away or try to keep alive by patching them up. But apparently, you can walk into a shop and buy them for five hundred quid now, just to be cool.

ALL THINGS REMEMBERED

This is something I was thinking about race. Being half black and half white, I can look at that question from both angles . . .

Imagine you live in England in the . . . I don't know, let's say twelfth or fourteenth centuries, whenever the Crusades were on. Imagine you're living in Scunthorpe, and your grandad is out ploughing the field or doing whatever, sowing seeds in his village, when all of a sudden this boat turns up and all these black guys get out of it, with loads of clubs and axes, and just club you and beat you and drag you off, put you in chains and take you all the way back to Zambia, and incarcerate you and make you pick cotton.

It would be outrageous, wouldn't it? It would be like your whole family was torn apart. So how would you feel, sitting at home in Llandudno, when all of a sudden a boat hits the shore, and all these black guys get out – really angry black guys? Or maybe they're not so angry. They might be really lovely people who just want to shake your hand and be nice to you, and then maybe they give you a nice bottle of whisky. Or maybe they just say, 'I tell you what. I'll take all those lovely shiny pearls you've got, and I'll give you this microwave.' This microwave that you can't fucking use, because you've got no electricity to plug it into, so it's basically pretty much fucking useless. Would the whisky be any more useful than the microwave? Not quite sure. We'll work the science out later on, eh?

When you look at the question of race in the broadest sense, it's the story of all these different tribes starting out at the equator and then nomadically moving across the globe, and becoming

whiter and whiter as they get further away from the sun. Fast forward to centuries later, when these farthest-from-the-equator people have become educated in the Western sense, and that justifies them in their own minds in getting on a fucking boat, going back to the place which they'd originally come from, and then killing all your animals and then swapping you loads of fucking small shit like the whisky or the microwave for all of your incredible wealth. And that's before you even factor slavery into it!

What's unbelievable is that when they went back to Africa to rediscover it – unbeknown to them, or in denial about the fact they actually came from there in the first place – they did it in this rigid Western way of, 'Let's give you Christianity. There you go, let's give you Christianity, because if you don't have Christianity, you are going to burn in hell, and you will be God-fearing. Even if we have to kill you to get that message across.'

It's like a really bad game of football cards, isn't it? 'I'll give you this Division Four fucking defender for a really good striker in your Zambiki tribe.' Do you know what I mean? It's a bit of a bad deal: it's not a straight swap. 'We'll impose this religion on you which did not emerge organically from your culture and is going to cause an incredible amount of misery and pain because we can and will use it to justify doing whatever the fuck we want, and in return we'll take all of your gold and your diamonds.' Yeah, cheers.

I was watching that BBC documentary, *Black and British: A Forgotten History*, and looking at the section about the Asante tribe in Ghana (commonly known as the Ashanti), whose chiefs have to have a special helper to hold up their gold jewellery, because it weighs so fucking much. It's no accident that those guys look like Eric B and fucking Rakim. They were doing centrifugal casting! Their whole religion was based on gold and the fact that gold is a really beautiful, pure metal. You know, I have it in my fucking mouth, and after twenty-five or thirty years of having it in my mouth, it hasn't poisoned me, because it doesn't poison you, because it's pure. Did you know there are goats living on certain mountains that chew rocks which have certain composites of gold inside the rock, and when these goats die and they look at the skulls, there's actually gold leaf inside the fucking skulls, because they've eaten so much of it, it composites into their fucking bone structure? Fact! I've done my research!

When I think about how important gold has been in my life and why I would want to work on it and even make it a part of my body, I just keep going back to how much I love grills – the culture of them. As much as I love it, there's almost a sadness as well when I think about why people of black origin gravitate to gold. Because we came from it and it came from us. There were tribes of our people that wore gold ceremonially – who were dripping in it. And then the West came, and they tricked us out of the wealth of our gold with their sleight-of-hand whisky/

microwave magic. And so now we put it in our mouths to ensure that even when everything else is stripped away from us, we're still going to look cool.

So let's go back to imagining the twelfth or fourteenth century, and all of a sudden, you know, you're living in Scunthorpe and a boat turns up with three hundred black people on it with clubs and fucking guns and ammunition and they come on and they iron everyone out, take all their shit and get back on the boat. Now imagine if those black people in the twelfth and fourteenth centuries had Twitter and they had iPhones, and they went, 'Whoo hoo, let's film this shit while we go into this village and fuck it up!' and they actually filmed those atrocities.

So you go back to your Fred Flintstone village in the after-math, and you're watching the story unfold on your fucking Fred Flintstone fucking TV – there's all these Dino messages about what just happened, you know: 'It's a sombre scene today as we're standing on Llandudno beach, after these black people came on boats, and they landed, and they killed three thousand people in the village, they took all of the gold and the gems.' That would equate to a really big heist, wouldn't it? It'd be like breaking into the national bank . . . 'And they got back on the boat and fucked off with everything that wasn't nailed down, and now here we are, all the survivors in this village are cleaning up the macabre mess that they've made and the dead bodies and shit.' I mean, could you imagine that as a newsfeed?

Hey, didn't happen, right? But if you turn it the other way round, it did happen. And not in the twelfth or fourteenth century either, but it was still happening in the last century – in maybe more subtle ways, it's still happening in this one – and every street in Bristol and Manchester's still named after the fuckers that did it. And that's where all the money that paid for all the nice buildings in the TV costume dramas came from as well.

So I look at that whole situation with race, and the way that people of black origin have maybe been on the back foot a lot of the time. And I think, 'Well, it's no wonder, because of all of that trauma.' If you compare this situation with that of an individual person – maybe even a person like me, who goes through bad shit when they're a kid and spends their whole life trying to get over it – well, maybe everything makes a bit more sense. Because that imaginary newsfeed I was talking about not only exists, it's playing in our heads every day of our fucking lives.

So if you think about it from that angle, maybe when you come across some black kid just going, 'Fuck you, I want to be a rapper,' and deciding to just fucking spit about the 'hood and be aggressive all the time, maybe that's because they've had to be like that – in survival mode – the fight or flight switch has been Sellotaped fucking on from the minute they were born.

I find it quite weird that people can't get their head around the continuing relevance of these past atrocities. So long as it's post-Twitter and we can see it and it makes an impact, then we can really get uppity about it. But if it was pre-internet, 'Ooh, sorry, I'm not sure about that.' It's almost like people of black origin are not allowed to have a timeline in the modern world, which I think is ridiculous.

I had various art classes in my youth that really changed my life by giving me little glimpses of who I was going to be. One of them was when I was being moved around as a kid in a very turbulent situation. I was at Croxdene children's home in Bloxwich, waiting till new foster-parents could be found after my placement with Mr and Mrs Jones had gone up in smoke. I think I was between social workers at the time, too.

In the midst of all that chaos, I had this unbelievable art class. I arrived at my new but only transitional school in the afternoon – I can't remember the name of the place, but it was in Walsall – and they were in the middle of an art lesson. The teacher was very welcoming – 'Everyone meet Clifford, he's joining us, so make him feel at home' – then he gave me a piece of plasticine and said, 'Let's make something.' I sat at the back of the class and looked at my fucking hands – very young hands as they were then. I remember my palms were sweating because I'd been gripping them together so tightly while they made me stand at the front of the class and tell everyone who I was. My eyes had been fixed firmly on the floor because I didn't want to meet anyone's gaze. But then the teacher gave me this ball of plasticine, and I actually started to create something with it.

What I ended up making – and there's a TED talk online somewhere where I go into this in a lot of detail – was a fucking pram. One minute I was moulding the soft plasticine in my hands, then, the next thing I knew, the teacher was taking me back up to the front of the class, saying, 'Oh, it's amazing, Clifford, that looks so good, let's show everyone what you've done.' I remember him looking at me, and me kind of extending my arm with this beautiful little pram in my hand. There was the stylised little round head of a baby beneath the hood and a blanket covering where the body would've been. You would not need to be Sigmund Freud to see this was the work of a kid who was wanting to be mothered. But then as I held out this pram to show everyone, I felt this spurt of anger, and I squeezed it as hard as I could so it was destroyed, and then threw it down on the ground and ran out of the class.

People who have heard this in the past have responded to it as if it's a very sad story – which of course it is in a way. But the pram needed to be destroyed because I needed to find the man beyond the baby who was in there. In the long run, the excitement I felt about creating something would prove more enduring than the anger which drove me to crush it (though admittedly sometimes it would be a close-run thing). And from that point on I'd be drawing or making things whenever I got the chance. Once I got to my secondary school, Frank F. Harrison, there were glass cases in the art department that had sculptures in them. I quickly became fascinated by these sculptures, and the art teacher who showed them to me – Mr Hurst – would be an important figure in my life. So much so that I paid homage to him in a documentary I made called *The Alchemist*.

I was a surprise guest at his sixtieth birthday party, where I thanked him for giving me the opportunities that helped me to become an artist. He got me through my O level art exam, because I didn't really like drawing at that time, but he'd just say, 'Look, here's a fucking iron, there's a kettle, there's an ashtray, there's a newspaper, that's a window, that's the school over the road, that's a pikey fucking place there with caravans: draw it. We need you to do something.' That kept me in the game, but I passed because of doing sculpture – which I was really into. I made a bust of Stevie Wonder – with the glasses and the braids – which I put Zebrite Grate Polish on to give it a metallic look, even though it was actually a plaster cast. I was a plaster caster of the master blaster!

I bought *Songs in the Key of Life* recently, and listened to it all the way through, because I really wanted to see Stevie playing in Hyde Park, but I couldn't go. It still sounds beautiful, but sadly my sculpture didn't last so well. I was carrying it home after entering it in a competition when I dropped it. Never mind the sculpture, it was me who was destroyed that time. I think smashing that bust of Stevie was probably even more devastating to me than leaving my Bruce Lee kung fu swim bag at the bus stop when I was going swimming one summer.

One lesson I seemed to be learning in all these art classes was that it's easier to destroy things than it is to create them. There were a few other early creative mishaps that are funny in retrospect. Earlier on, when I was at Busill Jones primary school, I'd built this red racing car in the stock room. It was a term-long project, with a lot of very intricate wire-work and carefully painted cardboard. Unfortunately, once it was finished, it was too big to get through the door. Note to self: don't make art that's too big for the (door) frame!

Around the same time, I made an excellent Steve Austin-style bionic suit for a school production. That too had a lot of intricate workings painted on it – not unlike those biomechanical tattoos they do now. Unfortunately, when I had to run across the stage with it on, one of the rivets came undone and the leg fell apart. Everyone laughed at me, and I ran off the stage again. Note to self: you might think you're bionic but you're actually not.

My formal education in art would end in a similarly farcical way when, having just about got through a Foundation 1 art course in Walsall, I was starting Foundation 2 and they made us do life drawing in the nude. After we'd drawn this fat naked lady, they told us to take all our clothes off and then do it again. Something about the idea of getting undressed and sitting there with your art teacher didn't seem right to me – it just felt a bit perverted – so I walked out. Luckily, there were plenty of concrete walls in Heath Town, Wolverhampton, for me to learn my trade on.

This is an extract from a talk I had recently with my friend and mentor Gus Coral, who was the cameraman on the documentary Bombin'. *He has been a very important person in my life over the last thirty years – so much of a role model in terms of what a father should be that I often call him 'Dad' or 'Pops'. We recorded this conversation on the eighteenth floor of Dorney Tower, which is Gus's flat in Chalk Farm, where I lived right at the start of my music career – sleeping on a bed with Gus's films of Art Blakey stored underneath, maybe hoping that some of the knowledge they contained would seep into me by osmosis. The poster for the Blakey documentary* Father Time *on the back of the door definitely did, as that helped shape* Timeless.

Goldie: I think the point I'm trying to fucking get to, which has been eluding me, is . . . I don't know how long I can be switched on like this. Like, everything, at the same time. The kid, the girl, the flower, the petals – everything is all so *on*.

Gus: I know what you're feeling. I've felt like that for very short times, but it doesn't sustain, at least, not for me . . .

Goldie: And I don't think it can sustain without you 1) becoming really paranoid, and/or 2) jumping off a building. I'm definitely taking that into consideration with this new abnormal heart-rate thing I've found out I've got now. The first time it happened was in London about five years ago: it was one little blip, and I thought, 'Fuck.' I must have caned it one weekend or something, and it just happened on a Tuesday. So I went to Harley Street to see this doctor who I've had for years, and he went, 'Ah, how are you?' I said, 'I dunno, I've fucking got this little thing, you know?' 'I'll check you out.' 'Oh, it's a murmur, sometimes it happens, it's a murmur.' I'm like, 'It's fucking mumbling, someone mumbling behind me I don't know what about.'

He says, 'If it happens again, let me know.' Never happened again. Then, about . . . about six months ago, it started happening, just once, then twice . . . then three or four times a day, then it's starting to like . . . I think at its peak, fifteen times . . . and I went to see a doctor in Thailand, and I was actually lying down for the ECG with the woman and the nurse, the Thai nurse. I was lying back, and she . . . I felt it go, 'Oof,' and she went, 'Oh! Abnormal! Abnormal!' and, like, that's just not what I want to hear right now, in a foreign language: 'Abnormal! Abnormal!' And I'm like, 'Oh, fuck.'

So then I'm waiting for forty minutes. I call my wife Mika and say, 'Look, babe, they've found something, it's an abnormality.' Now, let's just face it, most of us—

Gus: Are abnormal!

Goldie: Are abnormal, and, let's face it, the other thing is that when I do get a fucking . . . if I get a headache, it's a tumour, right? You know, that's what I'm like. I've got a foot ache: my foot's going to fall off. So it didn't scare me: it petrified me. It's a real wake-up. This is mortality. Because, don't forget—

Gus: It shouldn't really, because you're mortal anyway!

Goldie: I know that, Dad, but you've got twenty years on me, Pops, come on! I'm just saying, for me, I'm the guy who gets anxious watching his fucking bollock hairs change to grey: one, there's two, there's three; pull one out, five come. I'm just seeing hairs turning grey, even in nostrils and beards, like, wow, this has gone grey overnight. I'm watching myself go, very slowly, and I'm just watching, very, very slowly, in this beautiful . . . fucking slow-exposure photograph, right? Because I'm already switched on, it's all alarm bells.

Anyway, I waited to see the doctor. The doctor comes. I go, 'Hi, Doctor, tell me how long I've got to fucking live, then. What's it going to be?' And he goes, 'Oh, no! No, no. First, you're not going to die, OK? You're not going to die, and you're not going to have a heart attack.' 'Ever, Doc, really? I'm going to live for ever? That's it!' I just saw my daughter Koko's face going, 'Yay!'

Gus: Who does that song, 'I want to live forever'?

Goldie: A few people. But anyway, so, he says this, and I'm like, 'OK, that's cool . . . it's nice to know.' I say, 'What the fuck?' He says, 'Yeah, this is the abnormality' – he shows me – 'but you have a really, really slow heart rate.' 'What do you mean, "slow"?' He says, 'Slow. It's 46bpm slow.' I said, 'What is that, is that good?'

Gus: It's all that 170bpm music you play!

Goldie: He says, 'It's really good.'

Gus: Athletes have that.

Goldie: You know what he said? He said, 'That's a gift of God – that's hereditary . . . that's your father, that's your bloodline.' But

ALL THINGS REMEMBERED

I'm thinking, 'OK, you've told me I've got a really fucking good heart rate, but how do we get rid of this fucking abnormality?'

'The thing is,' he says, 'we can't give you beta-blockers, which slow your heart down, because you'll die!' It's slow already. 'We can put a catheter up the vein in your artery and go to the heart and burn it out.' I'm like, *'Burn?* Burn my heart? I don't want you to burn my fucking heart; I've been burning my heart for years, I can't burn it any more!' So I ask the doc to explain it to me – 'What is it like?' He says, 'Well, let me draw the picture. You've got your big chamber, your electrical pulse charging your body and your life, pump, pump, pump, but then you've got a lower one in the lower chamber which puts out another pulse – we don't know how it happens, but it does.' I said, 'So it's like a young heart, pumping through an old heart?' He said, 'That's exactly it.' I went, 'That's good enough for me. Now, if I need a spiritual explanation, I've got one.'

So, in fact, since knowing that, when it happens I can kind of calm it down. Because I know it's there, I can just calm myself down. The doctor leans back in his chair and says, 'Well, do you smoke?' 'One a day, two a day.' 'Ah. Do you drink?' 'Once a month maybe I'll have a vodka blowout.'

Gus: You do yoga.

Goldie: 'I do yoga four times a week.' The doctor says, 'Oh.' Now he's frowning, and I'm thinking, 'What the fuck?' 'What about sleep?' 'Ha – sleep, that'll be it! I only sleep four hours.' He went, 'Ah, you've got to sleep.' Then he starts waving this prescription: 'We'll give you some sleeping tablets.' I'm like, 'I've done a lot of them, and I don't want to do any more of them.' So I'm going to start sleeping in the day. That's what I'm going to do. That's how I'm going to solve it.

Gus: Especially now you're living in a hot country, you take that kind of hottest part of the day and sleep through it . . .

Goldie: Well, I worked it out that if I can just have two sleeps, I can probably double the length of my life – by sleeping. That's mad, isn't it? But beyond that I think it's just a good way to rewire what really matters with the abnormality being . . . just give it a bit more space; there is a younger heart coming through an older heart, but that's just what self-reinvention is – it's another electrical pulse that I've created. I've created that, I've manifested that. It's not the dodgy ticker that's missing a beat here, it's not like it's missing two fucking beats. It's creating more, in fact. So it's like—

Gus: It's a little heart roll.

Goldie: I've got like a fucking snare roll going through, and it's a little cheeky fucking young one that you can sing along to – a little jazz snare. It's almost like the beat coming through from another DJ in a different room in a club.

Gus: I mean, you could draw that on an ECG. You know what that looks like, the ECG? I remember you doing a chart of music you were going to do at the Festival Hall. It looks a bit like that.

Goldie: I've already got it on an ECG. I've got it and it goes, 'Woah!'

A5. Jasper and the Red Go-Cart

So much happened when I was in Lew Joseph children's home that you wouldn't think one of the stories I'd remember most clearly would involve a cat, but it does. I was getting bullied a lot at the time and I suppose having this animal that I could play with meant a lot to me. His name was Jasper and he was a beautiful short-haired Russian blue. In a funny way, because he had these unusual green eyes, I felt that he had my eyes in his face.

It was Chris and Steph who had bought him, and they kept him more in their flat in the week, probably because there were too many kids around and he was just getting pulled from pillar to post. But at the weekend, when most of the other kids went home and I would be one of the small number left there with this kind of skeleton crew looking after us, I really got to play with him. I used to love getting him to chase balls of string, or hanging things down through the banisters on the stairs for him to jump at.

One winter morning, we were all having breakfast – probably thirty-five kids, all having boiled eggs, which I love to this day, and racks of toast. There is something about toast on a rack – the equal space of a centimetre between each piece, the way it goes slightly goes cold when it's been delivered, but when you put butter on, there's still this beautiful heat between the toast and the butter. It doesn't soak in too much, but at the same time it doesn't stay on the surface too much either – just enough – and it tastes the same now as it's always done: the bollocks.

Anyway, while we were having breakfast, Auntie Steph ran in screaming, but as she screamed, she kept putting her hand back up in front of her mouth. Uncle Chris ran out and he just kind of grabbed her and steered her back out of the room, and all the kids were like, 'What's going on? What's going on?' Chairs started moving and scratching the floor, and there was a big hoo-hah as kids were getting up, though I think Auntie Rhoda was saying, 'You've all got to sit back down, have your breakfast.'

Chris and Steph had shut the door behind them, but there was still this noise coming from where something was happening in the hallway. Steph was clearly inconsolable about something. Then Chris came in, and he pointed a finger to me, and said, 'Come here.' At that point, I thought, 'Oh God, what have I done now?' so I came out, really nervous, and feeling like my belly had sunk down past my knees. When I got there, Uncle Chris said, 'Look, I'm really, really sorry, but there's been an accident and Jasper's dead.' I was just destroyed. He put his hand on my shoulder and said, 'Look, it's going to be OK, but I need you to really help us here. Do you want to go and get Jasper?' I felt this moment of sadness, but also this moment of joy that I'd actually been asked to do something to help.

Towards the end of the previous summer, I'd done this kind of artistic project with Chris where we'd been making a go-cart. We got the wood sorted, and it was mine and his thing that we worked on together during the school holidays and the week-ends when other people were away. I'd put the big pram wheels on the back and small pram wheels on the front. But what was so beautiful about this go-cart was that I'd painted it red, and I'd sanded it down – because Richard at the garage, who was the guy I got a Saturday job off, told me, 'When you paint something, you've always got to sand it down and paint it again – if you do it twice, it'll be amazing.'

He was right, because we'd painted the go-cart this lovely bright, letterbox red, then let it dry and sanded it down and painted it again. And the finish *was* amazing. And you could steer the go-cart with this rope we'd threaded through the small wheels at the front. But winter came really quick that year, and because we were working on it in this outhouse, which was like a vegetable shed for the kitchen – you'd get the key and go behind Chris and Steph's Austin Allegro, which was always in the car park, to get in – it got too cold for us to quite finish the project. The go-cart had this beautiful flat top and red finish and pram wheels, but it didn't have any sides on it yet.

Anyway, so Chris said, 'Look, why don't you go and get Jasper? He's at the bottom of the hill, and you should maybe use the go-cart to carry him up on.' So I'd gone and got the go-cart out, blown a bit of dust off it, and all the kids were at the window as I was coming round the back to the right of the big building at Lew Joseph and up the driveway. On my way to get Jasper with the go-cart I remember lifting it up a bit 'cos I was going down-hill and walking with the wheels tilted to one side.

I finally got to the bottom of the hill, and there he was – Jasper. He was in the road, by the kerb, but he just looked like he was sleeping. The air was really cold and everywhere was white – Jack Frost had definitely been to call. I put the go-cart down and went to pick Jasper up. He still looked like he was only sleep-ing, but when I prodded him he was rock hard. I kind of peeled him off the tarmac and placed him on the go-cart, then I started pulling him along behind me as I walked back up the hill. Even though it was sad, I was still pleased because I felt like I'd been asked to do something important. Most of all, because Chris had asked me to do it. We got really close at some points. We'd draw a line across the grass with chalk and I'd play handball with him. The thing about Chris was he was so passive-aggressive towards me that I'd always be trying to impress him – whether it was by trying to get on his team when we were playing football, or in whatever way – but sometimes he'd just diss me. Looking back, I don't think he meant anything by it. He probably just worked really long hours and it must have been very claustrophobic for him and Steph living effectively 'on the job'. He and Steph had their own accommodation that was next to the TV room, which was next to the shoe room, then there was a long corridor leading to the main lobby. Then, to the right, was the play room, and the breakfast room, then there were these massive windows and concrete stairs that led up to the dormitories. Those were the stairs I'd hang things over the side of for Jasper to jump up for.

Anyway, I was pulling the go-cart back up this hill and tears were streaking my face and almost freezing on my skin 'cos it was so cold, and the bus we got to school in Willenhall (which was the same one we got to roller-skating) went past. I remember the wind of it passing me and I carried on up the hill till I got to the driveway at the top. All the other kids were there, and Chris and Steph, and Chris just looked at me really puzzled and said, 'Where's Jasper?'

So I turned around and looked back at the go-cart in horror, and Jasper wasn't there. I was beside myself. I didn't know where he'd gone, and Chris was going, 'Where's Jasper? What have you done?' And then he kind of pushed me to turn round and go back the way I'd come, and all the time I was thinking, 'What have I done?' And I was thinking about the way I painted the go-cart really well and sanded it back down and painted it again so it was really smooth and shiny. And then I was thinking about how fucking freezing it was and the fact that Jasper had been out there all night so all his insides had kind of sunk down inside him and when I'd peeled him off the tarmac he was like the underside of one of those toy plastic soldiers you'd have – completely flat.

So I'd placed him on top of the go-cart, which, as I said,

hadn't been finished in the summer so had no sides, and we'd been trundling up the road with the school and a big fence on my right-hand side. I would've had to have come down off the kerb and then go back up it, and it was probably at that point when Jasper slid off the top of the go-cart and back into the road. As luck would have it – and this was one cat whose nine lives had certainly run out – it turned out that the bus I'd felt the wind from had run over him again.

So Jasper had been double-ended by this bus and things were not looking good for him, overall. Chris just told me to go back to the home and then he picked Jasper up, tucked him under his arm and carried him up the hill while I did a walk of shame past the other kids and back into the children's home. It was all very frosty, just like the morning – 'Just get your shit and go to school and we'll talk about this later on.' There didn't seem to be much forgiveness going on. As a result, even though I didn't kill Jasper, it kind of felt like I did. There wasn't just the trauma of him dying but also the guilt complex because I'd been given one job to do and I'd completely fucked it up.

As terrible as all this was at the time, it's fucking hilarious now. Obviously the interesting question in hindsight is: would Jasper have still come off the go-cart if I'd only given it one coat of paint? My search for perfection within a chosen art form had certainly backfired in this case. Luckily, that would never happen again . . . or would it? Either way, I did love that cat . . . that dead cat.

A6. The Dorian Gray of Fucking Breakbeat

So where am I? Going to the 2017 *NME* Awards at Brixton Academy, that's where; thinking back over some of the gigs that have happened there, right through the whole history of British music. Like the time I was DJing as a support act for the Sex Pistols' reunion tour in 2008. I collected £38 in 2p and 10p coins, and even the odd £1 (which must have come from people with more money than sense), thrown by a crowd of disgruntled punk fans who didn't like fucking drum 'n' bass music.

When you're catching coins in your baseball cap while another one whistles past your ear, you can't help thinking, 'Come on, sunshine, you guys seem to have forgotten what punk's all about: it's meant to be about setting the fucking cat among the pigeons, isn't it?' That's what drum 'n' bass was, too – a different way of channelling the same impulse to give the system the middle finger. But drum 'n' bass was punk without the voice, so the resonance of the sound itself was doing the work, and the way that conveyed the emotion of how we felt was almost like fucking Braille.

Part of me realised that one reason John Lydon and the guys had said, 'Goldie, we want you to come and support the tour,' was because they knew their crowd were going to be very, very angry about it – 'We want them to be upset before we come onstage.' 'Job done, thank you very much.' Next time they should just play '(Is This the Way to) Amarillo' – they might get an even better result.

Another part of me was never going to just lie down and take it. I thought, 'I'll tell you what, I want to fucking stick the knife in: I'm going to play Public Image Ltd – John Lydon's solo

project, which all Pistols fans fucking hate – because this is pissing me off now.' So while everyone was throwing coins at me waiting for the Pistols to come onstage, I was playing them PIL, which had been the end of the story the first time around. That's what I call being a proper fucking upstart!

Anyway, the point of going back to the *NME* Awards and doing the red carpet for the first time in ages is to announce that I have a new album – *The Journey Man* – ready to be released later in the year. It's good, after being away from the UK in Thailand for a while, to see how people still look at me, as if I put them on edge a bit when I talk to them.

Someone says, 'Fuck me! You don't age.'

'Yeah, I know. I'm Benjamin fucking Button. I'm also the Dorian Gray of fucking breakbeat: I keep a very grotesque fucking portrait of me locked away in chains in a fucking room, and every time I bring one EDM motherfucker down to his knees, the picture gets a little bit more beautiful!'

Technically, I'm there to hand out an award for Best Female Artist, where twenty years before I was being given a BRAT Award for Best Dance Act. Twenty years ago! Go figure that: I'm still here now, as ruthless as ever with my viewpoints, and even more clear about how I feel about the industry. So I go out onstage and I say, 'Listen, guys – twenty fucking years ago I was given this award . . .' and the *NME* Awards at that time, you have to remember, were almost a piss-take of what was going on in the overground, in terms of them saying, 'We're going to have our own fucking awards, because you lot ain't listening to what's going on in the real underground . . .' Obviously, part of that was just their way of defining their own position, but it worked out well, so God fucking bless you, *NME*. I still have that award today; it's a middle finger sticking up.

So this time around I say to the crowd, 'Look, I want you guys out there to give it the fucking middle finger – show me your fucking middle finger like a junglist would show you the fucking lighter in a club,' and half of them start putting their fingers up, but the others are a little too conservative and would really rather not.

Now it's grime that they're saying is the new punk. The *NME* always have to say things are 'the new punk' – it's the only way they can feel like they understand them, and I get that. It makes more sense with grime, too, because the angry voices are there, so in a way the echo is clearer to pick up than it was with drum 'n' bass. But let's not forget where we've come from. It's an evolution, the same way poster art is an evolution from graffiti. But you can't understand the later one without understanding the earlier one.

At the peak of graffiti in New York, when the best subway art was being made, if you look at great pieces like *Children of the Grave* by Dondi, and some of the stuff Seen did, do you know why those pieces happened? Because they had two weeks – even three weeks – in the yards, because the New York subway system at the peak of summer was on strike, in a fight with New York's council and the mayor's office. The unions stopped the trains, so all the cats and the blues brothers and the fucking beautiful people in the Bronx, and the kids whose moms were on fucking angel dust and whose dads were on fucking crack, so their mothers and fathers have fallen away and the streets were now their parents – the gangs and the crack and violence became the father, and the art became the mother – they went in there and they painted those fucking trains. Because they wanted to voice their opinions.

And do you know what? They weren't even saying, 'Put up our wages,' or 'Stop the fucking bomb.' All they were saying was, 'I have a fucking name' – 'My name's Dondi', 'My name's Seen', 'My name's fucking Lee', 'My name's fucking NOC 167', 'My name's fucking Style Wars'. All these guys wanted was to just say their names, because that's the only thing they'd fucking got – like dogs pissing on a lamppost. Except this lamppost was moving – put your name on the right train and it would carry your identity all the way through the tunnels from the Bronx to Queens. It was like the first internet.

Anyway, those guys had all the time in the world in those train yards. Because people didn't associate car paint with graffiti, they could steal the stuff by the shit-load, racking up cans and cans and cans. But flash forward a few years, and all that's changed. Big Brother's got the upper hand and CCTV cameras are watching you. At that point you saw what's beautiful about the way culture adapts, because people who'd been getting advertising shoved down their throat 24/7 in the city their whole lives started thinking, 'We can advertise art in another way – cut and paste, poster art, do it graphically, prepare it on a computer, cut it out on a stencil, take it there, job done.' That's where someone like Banksy's been very fucking clever, because you go there with your stencil, bam, put it away and you're out of there.

The analogy works another way, too, because I think drum 'n' bass music did for electronic dance music in Britain what graffiti did for the art world in general. We kicked the fucking doors off and changed the fucking system completely. So when people are talking about 'grime this' and 'grime that', they are really talking about drum 'n' bass too, even if they don't know it. The people making the music know it – Dizzee (for me he stands alone, way ahead of everyone else), Kano, Skepta (who I've done a track with), and let's not forget the godfather of grime, Wiley. Me and Wiley have got a lot in common, and not just the fact that we're both a bit nuts.

I'm standing there talking to him and he tells me, 'Yeah, man, you're *our* godfather. You, Nicky Blackmarket, Ray Keith, you brought us in.' DJ Target from Roll Deep is standing next to him going, 'G, you know this,' and so he should be, because he was a fucking intern at Metalheadz, and now he's interviewing me on Radio 1. That's what I love about music – if you stay in the game long enough, some of the seeds you planted will start to come through.

You can't plant seeds on a candy road – the soil's got to be ploughed up for them to germinate, and that's why you need bad times as well as good times. It's got to be underground as well as overground. That's why grime is going to last – because it's been under the surface long enough. It came up on the back of garage and then it went back under the surface after the initial wave. And now you've got people like Stormzy and Skepta taking it on.

If you look at how grime grew out of the speed-garage thing – which in turn came out of drum 'n' bass and good UK soul – it's beautiful how that evolution happens. That UK garage vibe was like the lover's rock of grime, just slightly out of time, slightly out of sync – all those guys at fucking Twice as Nice on a Sunday night. Then next thing you know, bam! The more underground side of the garage raves turned into So Solid Crew getting to number one with '21 Seconds' and turning the music industry on its head by winning a fucking Brit Award. They and Oxide & Neutrino put their own twist on the garage thing and started having massive hits. Meanwhile, you've got 'With a Little Bit of Luck' on the poppier side and Wookie's 'Battle' – which was a massive tune – somewhere in the middle. Then, just as that original explosion is starting to dim out and slide away, the grime thing with Wiley and Dizzee bubbles up through it. Those guys were already there, but suddenly everybody noticed them.

Exactly the same thing had happened with drum 'n' bass: it came up on the back of rave and it went back underground. And we dug our fucking heels in – because we realised what was going to happen to the music when rave culture became 'Charly says'. Now I love my rave culture, but all of a sudden, I had to stop the helium. We had to change that slightly – bring that down, write original vocals: 'We're not fucking this, we're not that, we're something else.'

Suddenly jungle was coming up through Rage and Roast

– let's not fucking forget Roast, Ibiza Records, Kikman Records, 'The Snowman', Lennie De Ice, Bodysnatch, Ragga Twins, Rum & Black; sixteen-track tunes, these were tunes that were being looped by Londoners, northerners. This was like breakbeat culture that was rough, man – it was like yard music, it was like music being made in Jamaica, for me. It really was. We'd be cutting dubplates at Tubby's, you know, and then Music House mainly, sitting with Leon and his brother, which was obviously Wookie, and cutting fucking tune after tune – all of us from Navigator, from the Raw club on a Sunday night. You'd have M-Beat making tunes and sampling fucking Randy Crawford and fucking Anita Baker, and Shy FX killing it.

When it came to drum 'n' bass, I wasn't really looking at it so much from a ragga aspect but more on the hip-hop template coming out of America. I'd done the sound systems and the blues parties (which reminded people of Jamaican descent of coming from Jamaica and still having that connection) way back when I was going to the Half Moon Club opposite Whispering Wheels in Wolverhampton. But when I went to America I kind of missed out on the UK dancehall thing. I understood that this was where the music called jungle basically spawned, and the MCing over beats thing was something I respected, but what I was about was the sound of the B-boy – breakbeat culture was my musical roots. That's what I was breakdancing to the first time I went to New York. No vocals to speak of, just the funky James Brown drum loop and maybe the odd little fragment of 'Mary, Mary . . .'

From Can to The Meters it was all about the breaks, and the breaks were about a DJ at a block party in the outer boroughs of New York cutting two records together. Because when the economic crash happened within that city, all the blue-collar workers who built Manhattan went back into the 'hood, and all of a sudden there was a ghetto full of their kids who had nothing to do, and the gangs filled the vacuum with all these territorial battles, and the block parties were kind of the antidote to that – the mother to the father. All of these dispersed families – Dominican, Surinamese, American, Afro-Caribbean, Jamaican-Caribbean, Cuban – found a way to come together and it was a beautiful thing, and that's where hip-hop came from.

So let me recap: I'm up there onstage, giving out this award for Best Female Singer. And of all the people who come up onstage that night to hand out awards, it's the Mayor of London, Sadiq Khan, who gets the biggest shout from the crowd, God bless him. I see him in the hallway before this happens, and I say, 'We should speak,' and he says, 'Yeah, let's have a meeting,' and he passes me his card. His assistant's behind him – she passes him the card – and he tells her, 'Let's make that happen.' Then he goes onstage and gives Skepta an award. This is the fucking Mayor of London! Oh my God, how times are a-changing – for the better in this case. It's nice to be able to say that in the era of Brexit and Trump. But then again, is Trump that much different to some of the other fuckers who came before him? I'd say not. America's just saying exactly what it's been wanting to say for all this time, but now they're saying it openly, as opposed to saying it under their fucking breath.

It all comes down to that good old fucking racist joke, doesn't it? A black man moves into a really nice area, because he's earned it. And when he's going out to get into his car every day, his next-door neighbour, every time, under his breath, is going, '*Cough!* Nigger! *Cough!* Blackie! *Cough!* Nigger!' And one day the black man thinks, 'You know what? I'm fucking sick of this, I'm going to say something.' And he goes round to the neighbour's door and he knocks on it and he says, 'Listen, man, you know what? I've got to tell you, man, I know this is a predominantly white area, and I know it's out in the fucking sticks, and you live in these great fucking grand houses and you have a Ferrari, but I also have a Ferrari and a Bentley, and I'm sick of your racist comments.' And the neighbour replies, 'Woah, woah . . . now hang on a cotton-picking second.' That's the joke.

If you want to see Obama as the black man and Trump as the neighbour, then that's up to you. But to me it's no bigger a joke than the time thirty-five years ago when New York mayor Ed Koch decided to wage his war on graffiti. He tried to turn New Yorkers against each other by paying the boxers Hector Camacho and Alex Ramos a load of taxpayers' money to be on posters proclaiming, 'Take it from the champs, graffiti is for chumps.' (Irene Cara from *Fame* was in another one which said, 'Fame is seeing your name in lights, not seeing it sprayed on the subway' – it's all right for you, love, you've got that option.) These are the people who built your office, Mayor Koch, you idiot! They laid the tracks for the subway and built your subway system, and now they have no jobs and you're screaming from the top of your office about trying to eradicate graffiti? How fucking dare you try to deny these Cuban kids, these Colombian kids, these Afro-American kids their one avenue out?

Culture will never go away, however much some people might want it to. And so to see Sadiq Khan recognising that is very encouraging. Thank you, Mayor Sadiq. I hope you realise that we now need to make soundproofed clubs, and we need to make more spaces in London that are open for parkour or being painted openly by graffiti-writers. London is a canvas, and the city should be a canvas for the youth, because the streets of our inner cities are the universities and the halls of fucking disrepute, and of achievement and of failure, and of greatness. We need to fucking soothe these kids' pain and we need to support them, because society is a very loose bike-chain that's coming off all the time. And what it needs is people like Sadiq to make that bike-chain a little tighter – to take out a few links and put it back together, to ensure the back wheel and the front are actually in sync – so we don't have the latency that causes the effect. Because we've lost enough of our children.

This isn't some Stephen Lawrence shit that you can just fucking sweep under the carpet and hide, and then all of a sudden, twenty years later, say, 'We had them bang to rights, after all.' Oh, no shit, Sherlock! Right now London is like the splintered boroughs of New York: Brixton, for me, is like fucking Brooklyn; Hackney and Dalston are like Queens; and west London's like the fucking Bronx. That's what it's like for me. It's the same shit, but then at the same time it's not, because when you had the London riots back in 2011 you'd see the guys sitting on YouTube with a fucking scarf round their face going, 'Yeah, man, it's just fucked up here, where we're living . . .' And I'm thinking, 'You're wearing £300 trainers, mate, and your fucking jacket's worth a few bob, and you've got a fucking nice flat. I get you, mate, but you've got to put it in perspective. Have you ever been to São Paulo? Have you seen the 'hood in fucking Brazil? Have you been to the fucking Bronx?'

Of course, it's a bit different now, because the Bronx has gone through gentrification, the same way drum 'n' bass has. If you look back to that time which was the beginning of everything for me – when hip-hop culture came over from New York to the Shaw Theatre in London in 1982, and I met Afrika Bambaataa, and the graffiti artist Brim Fuentes (who was my God and kind of still is) saw me and we got on – at that point the Bronx was kind of on fire.

Brim said to me, 'I want to go up north, I want to see Manchester, I want to see Liverpool.' And Brim Fuentes, from the Bronx, had seen what had happened in the Toxteth riots and in Birmingham when they were on fire, and he said, 'This is what fucking happened, man, this is what happened in the Bronx. It's great coming here, seeing you guys celebrating graffiti and the way that happened, but it's going to get fucking bad, man. The government's going to squeeze your shit, man, it's going to happen, man, before you know it.'

Now, thirty-five years later, I'm looking at Sadiq Khan trying to do the right thing and I'm thinking, 'God forbid we will have to be on fire before we make the right change in the housing situation, and stop making fucking rabbit burrows full of speed bumps and fucking bollards to stop everyone getting out of there.' You're making a fucking hornets' nest, you silly cunts! You're blocking up holes in what you call a rats' nest that's going to fucking explode. And I'll tell you why I know that: because I'm a fucking rat, if that's how you want to label me. Yeah, I am. I'm a fucking street rat. I'm proud of it. Because the last time a fucking rat made some fucking money it was Mickey Mouse. And that was Disney.

Oh, I know what you're saying – 'But, Goldie, that was a mouse . . .' Yeah, but it kind of looked like a rat, didn't it?

SIDE B

B1. Tales of the Hoffman Process I

To introduce the Hoffman Process, I'd say it's one of many ways of dealing with addiction, and a place for modern souls who are sick of the past – not just their own past, but also past ways of dealing with the addiction and other psychological issues. It could be you're into alcohol, it could be you're hung up on your grandad. Either way, the issue's the driver. And while I know that old-school rehab works for some people, it didn't work for me.

God bless you, Eric Clapton, but can I have my fucking eighteen grand back, you twat? Because that's how much it fucking cost me to go to your rehab place in Antigua – all for some fat cunt trying to whip me for his sins because I don't want to cross the fucking road every time I see a pub. Sorry, sunshine, but that ain't the fucking modern world right now. And, Eric, you set this place up, so as far as I'm concerned your rehab place should be responsible enough to answer the emails of customers who paid in full and are not too fucking happy with what transpired.

I've flown out to Antigua and I'm talking to some of the guys there, asking, 'Have you been here before? Because I'm new to this.' The alarm bells should've started ringing as soon as they told me, 'Oh, it's my third time, and I'm still sprinkling crack on my fucking cornflakes.' Or words to that effect. Not to make fun of other people's addictions, but that isn't me, guys. First and foremost, I can't do gear before fucking nine o'clock (at night, not in the morning), and once I see daylight, I'm back under that fucking rock. I'm not the kind of person that goes on a five-day bender.

But I decide to give it my best shot anyway. Then I turn up one fucking minute late for a session and this Midwestern cunt who's taking it decides that he wants to embarrass me in front of everyone. He tells me, 'Go back to your room,' like I'm a fucking nine-year-old. Then he comes to my fucking room and tries to barge his way in. I tell him, 'You come through that fucking doorway and I'm fucking ironing you out.' And he does come through it, and I do iron him out.

Then he calls the security, and the security are Jamaican, and I'm like, 'Yo, tell this pussy-claat to fucking move or I'll kill him' – patois, straight up. Family: done. But because this American guy can't understand the dialogue, he's lost, he's like, 'I'm going to call the other police.'

I was in Eric Clapton's rehab place for three days, and then I was gone. It works for some people, especially people who are maybe stuck in the seventies and eighties, but for me, there have to be new ways of dealing with this shit – fame, money, cars, women, drugs; all the big problems of life. And I think that as far as I'm concerned the Hoffman Process is that way.

So my mother is riddled with cancer, and she's not going to be OK this time. The doctors in the hospital give her six months to live and tell us, 'There's nothing we can really do, let's get her back home.' So we do that, but then I have to go off and do two fucking gigs up north, and that's when I get the call from my brother, Stuart, saying, 'She's going, mate . . . she's going to go tonight.' So my driver Fritz, who's a top boy, says, 'Come on, get back in that fucking car – let's get you up there.'

When we reach my mum's bedside in the Midlands, my brother Melvin's there. Now me and Melvin have had a few issues over the years, to put it mildly. It wouldn't be right for me to go into too many details here, but do I blame him for all of the shit that's gone down? He lived with my mother all those years, and he watched her pain. He watched her getting beaten up by the black men she fell in love with. He watched the fucking robbing, he watched everyone getting fucked up. Do you blame him? I can't blame him. I forgive him. Yeah.

Anyway, my little brother Stu is there too, and all the grand-kids. I sit with them, and my mother holds on all fucking night. Then, at about ten o'clock in the morning, her tongue goes black and her breathing changes. And she fucking dies. Chokes on her own vomit, convulsing, with her mouth open.

I've never told anyone the full story of what happened next, but I'm going to do it now. I should say first that, to me, from the moment my mother died, there was no sense of any of her being left behind. In terms of the body that remained, my thoughts were, 'That's not my mother. She's gone. Note to fucking self.'

A couple of days after her death, I had gigs in New York and LA that I decided not to cancel, because I thought, 'Am I going to sit around with a corpse on a slab, or am I going to do what my mum would want me to do?' So I flew to New York, got in there at about 9 p.m., and stayed in a hotel just outside of town, near the airport. Then I woke at three in the morning and said to reception, 'Guys, I need to get into fucking town. I need to get to Manhattan. Is there a train?'

Luckily, there was. So I got to the station at Union Square at about five in the morning, and I walked across 44th Street to West and 49th Street, and went to the Midtown Bikram yoga studio. I sat outside till it opened and then walked upstairs and found Geraldo, the guy taking the class. I'd been to a few classes with him, and when he asked me what was up, I just let it all go – burst into tears and hugged him, almost squeezed him to death, in fact. Good job I didn't, because I needed to be in that class.

At this point I was very much taking my inspiration – and gathering my strength – from a guy called Paul Dobson. He is my teacher at Sohot Bikram Yoga, in Clipstone Street in central London, who is also kind of my guru. Paul is a Leicester lad, and he'd told me a story I always remember about when his mum died. He was in Miami at the time and he had quite a rock 'n' roll lifestyle in those days, but as he walked past the Bikram studio on 14th Street, he kind of really saw it in a way he never had done before. He went in there and did yoga for the first time, then he went back the next day, and the next, and the next, and never looked back from then on.

So I did this class, and as I walked back towards the station at 44th Street – I remember I was wearing a pair of flip-flops, which was not very urban of me – the weirdest thing happened. This stocky fucking Boston builder-type of guy pushed past me.

So I just fucking pushed back. He was shocked and said, 'What the fuck?' But I just said, 'Fuck you!'

'What did you say?'

'Fuck you! Fuck you! Fuck you!'

At that point, the guy put his hands up to fight – a signal I would've normally known how to respond to, but in this case I didn't put my hands up in response. I just kind of held my stance and backed away towards a wall – in my flip-flops. He was like, 'Come on, you pussy,' and I knew he was going to start punching, but I just started smiling, and I protected my face, and he did start punching – over, under, bam, bam – and I kind of fell back against the wall thinking, 'I'm dead here.' He carried on punching for a while, but pretty soon he was out of breath, and I just pushed him away, said, 'Fuck you!' – once more for luck – and walked off.

As I walked, I could feel the lumps coming up all over my head and body, but even while that was happening, I felt good. I knew my only options had been either do what I did or go and find some drugs in a bar, which I didn't want to do. I got the train to the airport all swollen up, my face was hot like a radiator, but all the way I was thinking, 'I got punched, kid. Well done.' It was just something primal that I needed to do. It wasn't just about resisting the urge to meet violence with violence, it was also about accepting the pain. I just wanted to get smacked in the face – like some fucking businessman in the West End who wants to pay a fat bird to lie on him. Was that too much to ask? The guy – who was probably forty-five, fifty, but with lots of beans in him – inflicted the pain to the point where he was out of breath, and then I was free to move on.

It was like the elastic bands had broken off – these big things that attached me to my mother, the one person I'd probably been most attached to. So I got the plane to LA, meditated, played a three-hour DJ set with 'Mother VIP' at the end, cried like a baby again, and flew back to the chapel of rest in the West Midlands.

In we go: 'Goldie, so pleased to see you. Sorry for your loss. Cup of tea, sir?' 'Love a cup of tea.' Cup of tea comes. I open the sliding doors, and there she is – my mother, no longer her, more like a little white monkey with skin stretched all over her body. I think, 'You're like a piece of marble.' And then I do something which is probably going to seem a bit strange.

My mum had said she wanted the full-length version of my track 'Mother' from *Saturnz Return* played at her funeral. Unfortunately, dear Maggie, note to self: 'It's too fucking long.' We didn't want to kill all the mourners with boredom. But still, it was something I'd agreed with her that I would do after her death, and I wasn't going to let her down. So I put the iPod headphones on and listened to the whole thing, sitting next to her corpse. Those were the longest sixty minutes of my life . . .

B3. 'Hammerwich the Haunted'

This is a poem I wrote about my time in the West Midlands children's home called Hammerwich.

Huge sweeping staircases with black underneath,
The smell of old mould, it would give you the creeps.
The sound of old ghosts in that Hammerwich home,
Pool tables, old lockers and sitting alone.
Old church classrooms, filled with big, fat bullies.
I'm so glad I'm small, so rolled up they won't even see me –
Hedgehog style,
With a smile.
I must remember I'm breathing.
'Wash your hands for tea,' all twenty-five of you ran.
It's panic and mayhem,
The toothpaste, the crayons,
Jesus will save us, especially on Sundays.
I'll give you my mother's address, but I don't know where
    she is.
Isn't it good to know Starsky and Hutch exist,
And that bacon and eggs comes from pigs?
What if, what if, what if
I could walk through walls, levitate or disappear,
Turn into a glass ball or a TV,
Or melt doors?
Who was that boy with one front tooth?
He was really, really nice to me, and he always told me the
    truth,

That he wouldn't be here for much longer, and he would be
  going away,
To live with his old uncle, he said, his name was Trevor.
He never left my mind,
Because I cried a lot that day.
Hammerwich the haunted, the creepy-crawly,
The place with the stairs for the boys that were naughty.

B4. The Text-Message Theory of Infinity

The first thing I want to say at the start of this chapter is, 'Let's not have any poo shame about who we really are.' You know what poo shame is? When you're a kid and you've put skid-marks in your pants and you hide them somewhere . . . they will get found.

The second piece of information I need to put out there is that if you can grasp the concept of infinity – something that has no end – then stick with me. Otherwise, there's a free pass to skip to the next chapter. It's like a customs form you'd fill out on a plane. Are you a resident of infinity? No? Then skip to section 3b.

My theory of the universe is just that – a theory, the same as everyone else's, but at least I admit it (unlike a few religions I could mention; in fact, all of them). So of course what follows is subjective as fuck, but I think it's viable – at least, it is to me . . .

I believe in infinity. Infinity is a child. Infinity realises it's a child, infinity is giving birth to the universe. Infinity's conscious. Infinity yawns, explodes, birth. OK, guys, game's up. You're driving me mad. You want a planet? There it is. You want man? You want woman? OK, there you are.

I think man's ignorance in the very first instance is that he sometimes forgets that he comes into this world head-first through a vagina. A lot of guys – myself included – forget that too often. But I think once you embrace the female aspect of existence, you realise that everything comes from this birth of the universe, this mother of worlds, giving birth in the spark of consciousness when it first began.

For me, the Big Bang was like the first thought that brought the universe to that consciousness, like the dream you're having just as you wake up. And I think of the battles that go on within the universe – between the forces of light and dark, yin and yang, male and female – as being very similar to the ones that go on in my own heart and mind, except obviously on a much grander scale.

Because as children of Mother Earth – or God, or whatever you want to call it – what she says to us is, 'You can have all the big boy's toys you like, all the exoskeleton of status and possessions and machinery, but when this life is done, it's all coming back to me.' The universe is just a larger organism that I am a part of. And when this body dies and these two hearts finally stop – hopefully one lasts longer than the other – then I'll simply return to the energy from whence I came.

The idea that our consciousness is just energy shifting from one place to another within the realm of infinity takes a bit of getting used to, but once you've managed to do that, it's very helpful. Especially if you're someone who has sometimes struggled to keep things in perspective.

Now this is the point where I want to take things a little bit out there with some ideas that are my own beliefs, which I know not everyone else shares. Because when you talk about past lives in interviews with *Noisey*, people do start to look at you like you're David fucking Icke. But this ain't no conspiracy theory lizard shit. All I'm asking you to think about are some interesting possibilities.

Because I do believe in past lives, and an afterlife which is yet to be decided. So if I can just gather enough positive energy within this current existence, when the moment comes for me to leave it, maybe I might be able to actively move into another realm. I've been tinkering around on the edges of past lives ever since a conversation with a shaman who was sticking needles

ALL THINGS REMEMBERED

in me for five-element acupuncture to treat my addiction. So imagine if there is another level of this fucking matrix which we can consciously switch on. Perhaps this life that is the one we remember the most is just the booting up of our circuitry before we leave our bodies behind and go beyond ourselves into another place.

OK, a few of you out there are possibly thinking, 'Fucking hell! G's lost it this time,' but please allow me to try to explain. I think the best way to do that is to say: imagine someone sends you a really beautiful text message, but then your phone battery dies and you don't get the chance to recharge it for a whole week. Now that phone doesn't have any blood in it, or any living organs, but it has a memory card and a chip made up of components which are somehow storing memory. So when you charge up that phone and switch it on and that text arrives, it's a delayed message from the past which has been stored in a component which is as cold as fucking day.

Well, maybe the universe has been storing my memory from all the past times I've been here in exactly the same way, so I'm effectively born into this life as a text message from the past. The point I'm trying to make is that I think I'm a little bit more complicated than a phone – even a smart one. Everyone is. We are the perfect computer, the killer hard drive, the MacBook Pro and beyond, and that's before you even think about the nano-technology we're hurtling towards, which will enable us to do astounding things with the human body because we understand it more.

Now, you can't ever finally get to the bottom of all the components that Mother Universe created, because she is infinite, but who's to say what kind of energy could be stored within my own organic electrical circuitry? What I do know is that we keep this energy in a place we do not understand. And once we lose some of that ego which is an aspect of the human condition that really holds us back, maybe it'll be possible for us to just become part of the oneness.

Over the next twenty, thirty, even forty years, if I'm lucky, I'm hoping to come a bit closer to doing that. One thing that I do know is the truth of the old Chinese proverb, 'Whatever we fucking think it is, it is not that name' – well, that's my translation anyway. The answer will not be what I first thought. I guess this brings us back to the shifting of the energy again. Maybe the same spirit travels through different lives, just like different art forms can channel the same creative impulse. For the moment, I'm a spiritual being having a very human experience, but in the future, who knows?

B5. Marc and Dego – My Two Miyagis

Mark 'Marc Mac' Clair and Dennis 'Dego' McFarlane have made music under many different names, but they're most widely known as 4 Hero, and their studio in Dollis Hill was the best university I could ever have attended as far as the sounds that became known as drum 'n' bass were concerned. That upstairs room right next to the tube station made the single biggest contribution to my musical life of any place I've spent time in.

I'd love to be able to remember exactly what I was thinking the first time I went up that tight little staircase. I think Suede might have been rehearsing downstairs, but this wasn't going to be a Britpop thing, at least not except in a broader sense of that word which no one would ever use. I went in and talked to Dego about the Ajax Project tracks I'd done with a kid called B in Iceland, then he played me some loops over this little sixteen-track mixing desk (which was big to me at the time), and we were just playing around with some ideas and recording them onto a DAT, then putting that back into a channel so it was layered.

Learning about layering sound was a big part of what that experience was about for me, and it was also about layering people. Dego would be there in the day and then Marc Mac would come in at about five o'clock for the nightshift, so for me it was like Dego was always on the side of jazz and Marc was always into the darker stuff. I think that's why when you listen to the music I made as a result of the time I spent with them – pieces like 'Angel' or 'Inner City Life' that would end up being on my album *Timeless* – the tunes always got turned over, back and forth between light and dark. Because that's who these guys were to me – and I suppose maybe also because that reflected the two sides of my own nature.

Without even thinking about it, they were almost turning me into this kind of Terminator character (I suppose that's what my track with that title is about, really – that and the fact that I was watching the film a lot at the time). Because all the months I was there with Marc and Dego, I'd also be going out clubbing – to Rage every Thursday, and beyond that to fucking Plumstead, Lydd airport, Ibiza Records warehouse parties – whereas they wouldn't, really. Marc and Dego weren't into raves; it just wasn't their thing – they were part of a more localised culture of sound systems and sound clashes.

So what I ended up with was these two worlds that I felt very comfortable in – this studio interior in Dollis Hill, Willesden, where all this amazing music with its roots deep in blues and soul and jazz seemed to live, and out and about in town where all the new stuff was going on. Marc and Dego would go out into that world too sometimes – they'd go to do these PAs at the Astoria or wherever, but afterwards they'd come back to the studio straight away to get on with whatever they were doing. So I was much more involved in all that external stuff which they weren't part of but their records were, because all the DJs were playing them. I wasn't an ambassador, or a custodian, or an observer, or an avatar, but there was a little bit of all those things in it, and Marc and Dego's energy would channel itself into the music I made under my own name. They taught me everything I know – it was a total *Karate Kid* thing, except with two Mr Miyagis.

B6. The 'Séancic' Method

Sometimes the word you need doesn't exist yet, so you just have to invent it. I do that all the time – it's like experimenting with different graffiti letter styles, except with meaning instead of shapes and colours. That's what language is all about, after all, because if people hadn't done that in the first place, there wouldn't be any fucking words at all, would there?

'Séancic' (I reckon you'd pronounce it, roughly, *say-aunt-sick*, and I guess my word is law here) is one of my favourites. Look as hard as you like for that one in the dictionary and you won't find it. It's the word I use to describe how I work. The Séancic Method is where you use other people to vicariously raise the spirits – the deities even – that you want within the music. I'm not the first one to do it, either. Duke Ellington's not playing the trumpet solos himself, is he? Phil Spector's not banging the kettle drum. Captain Beefheart's not got a guitar in his hand – he's locking his band up in a house and teaching them *Trout Mask Replica* by hypnosis.

What I do is the same thing, only by no means having their greatness and – at least at first – by electronic means. I made a choice with music, very early on, that I was always going to be looking over the shoulder of some other guy, watching technology – my eyes would be on the screen as he'd scroll up vertically through Creator, which was a program Marc and Dego and a lot of other people used, and I never really wanted to. I think that thread of 'not wanting to' goes back even earlier than that. Maybe it's a Freudian thing, but technology to me is the velvet claw, and I need to keep it at one remove.

I can't work alone. I can't read music, I refuse to engineer or produce. Why would I want to do that when I can sit with two engineers in a studio and bend them inside out until I've exhausted all the technologies that they have, until all the samplers are full and there's no more room? How am I going to conjure this out of them? By being the Doris Stokes of drum 'n' bass, that's how. And once I've got the spirits in the room, I'm going to make them dance to the tune I always wanted to hear. Because I know what's going where from the start, the picture's already done in my head, and all I have to do as an artist is keep the water clear.

The B-boys showed me the way, as they always do. As a graffiti writer, you have an outline, and that outline's in black and white, but in your head it's in colour. So when I say I'm going to play a chord, and I'm singing a chord in my head, to a musician they'll be like, 'Well, that chord is made up of twelve different chords, there's twelve different variations of that.' Whereas to me it's more kind of, 'This is the kind of chord that I like, just the sound of it.' By allowing us to change the pitch and texture and tempo of sound synthetically, electronic music obviously opens up enormous new possibilities for someone working in this way. It allows me to take a block of something and merge it with a block of something else – often recording my own voice, the natural first melody I feel in that moment – to create a special kind of melancholy that doesn't detune but somehow stays in key.

There are no Ouija boards involved, but that doesn't mean there's nothing supernatural about it. People say there aren't any ghosts any more. I think they've been phased out by fucking radio waves – that's why we don't see them as much, because the radiation has knocked us out of kilter and we no longer resonate at the same frequency.

I've heard and seen some strange shit over the years, that's for sure. I've definitely seen a dark entity – even though the exact nature of that entity was undetermined I definitely felt it was connected to certain people in my past life. And I've definitely seen Kemi on the end of my bed. I've felt the mattress be pushed down by her weight when she sat down on the end of it, which is weird in itself because you'd think of ghosts as being weightless.

What's that you're saying? That you don't believe in ghosts? What about your fucking iPhone 7 message, or the voice text your Edge phone sent you? So that's not a ghost, is it? Take it from me, if it's coming through the air and I can't see it, but it's there, it's information, then it's a fucking ghost. Don't start me with that can of worms! Take your smartphone back in time a few hundred years and try to use it and see how warm a reception you get. They'll be heating up the bonfire to burn you at the stake before you can say 'three-month contract'.

My cleaner in Thailand has sadly just lost her sister, whose name was Jessica. She died in a freak accident on a visa run, and strange things happened that week. My wife Mika's mother Nobuko clearly saw Jessica coming out of the fucking jungle, with a message that she didn't want to be on the metal: basically she meant she didn't want to be where she was in the hospital on the slab. She didn't want to be there, and who can blame her? Then she asked where her sister was.

When I told Jessica's sister what had happened, she burst into tears, but she also felt a slight relief. Mika's mum is Japanese, and she has that very spiritual aura about her that a lot of Japanese people have. Let's just say that if you were a ghost, you couldn't pick a better person to go to. In fact, if a load of aliens landed their spaceship in a field next to Nobuko's house, she'd probably just go out there and ask them if they wanted a cup of tea and how many sugars they take. Then she'd tell them about the fucking Korean market, and how cheap it is. She's that kind of woman: nothing fazes her – which is maybe how you'd need to be if your daughter was planning to marry me.

Anyway, I think the whole point of this is that I think that Jessica's spirit went to Nobuko – who is downstairs right now in the bedroom in the treehouse in Thailand – because she wouldn't want to go to Mika, because she didn't want to freak Mika out. Obviously Mika and Koko sleep with me in the bed. And I think Jessica's ghost didn't want to wake her and then of course frighten Koko.

Ghosts have got a lot of time on their hands for communicating shit to people. When you think about how often the living say, 'Oh, I just thought about you . . .' well, of course you probably thought about that person anyway, because do you know how many thoughts we can have in a fraction of a second? Then imagine how many it is in ten minutes. Just test it for yourself. Go to your iPhone, or whatever you have, put the stopwatch on, and forget about it for ten minutes. Then when you remember – 'Oh, shit, that's eleven minutes' – just think back to yourself about everything you did and all the thoughts you had in the intervening time. I guarantee you, it'll be a lot.

Try to be honest with yourself, and you'll be fucking surprised that your train of thought is both positive and negative, yin and yang, fire and ice, brutal and kind. If you're anything like me, there'll be a lot of other people's voices audible on that train. I have voices in my head all the time. There are constantly at least twelve people in my brain who I'm always speaking to, and sometimes arguing with. And who's to say all those people are actually technically alive?

I've always been fascinated by what the ghost in the machine might be, and how those ghosts can make themselves heard through music – not just David Sylvian's music, everyone's. The best way to let those voices have their say is definitely by the Séancic Method, to raise the deities and swirl like dervishes. But in the present.

SIDE C

C1. The Beautiful Accident

So where am I? It's March of 2006, and I'm in this Channel 4 TV show, *The Games*, knowing that I need the money to pay for my divorce, which is costly. It's the last day of six weeks' training and I'm thinking, 'This is fucking easy.' Jade Jones – from Damage, who's been Emma Bunton aka Baby Spice's fella for ever – was the only brother that could've taken me on. I was looking at everyone else thinking, 'All pussies, man, we'll smash this up easy.' Money in the bank!

Skating? Done it. Ice-skating? Piece of piss. Snowboarding? That's easy. Ego? Full throttle, 200 per cent. Me and Jade are mashing it up every week. Last fucking day and it's water-skiing. Down in Chertsey. I'm jumping, landing, bam! Jumping, land-ing, bam! Done it twice and this is the third and final run – the last time before the show airs in three days' time. It's like the dress rehearsal. Goes fine. Smooth as silk.

At this point, my manager (well, he's my ex-manager now, but he was my manager then) turns up – 'Just go around again.' 'No.' 'Come on, let's go out again.' Of course, the ego's kicked in, hasn't it? 'All right.'

This is going to be impressive, isn't it? Because he's in the boat. It's pulled me up out of the water. The skis are too tight but it's OK. I've crossed the wake fine. I put my heels into it and come right round – hit the edge of the ramp, you need to pull away so you get the most traction. Now I've launched off it. The jump is beautiful, it's amazing, it's better than Eddie the fucking Eagle, baby. I've landed, dug my heels in, and the wake's caught the skis, pulled the leg under the water and snapped it.

The only way I can describe the feeling of a leg breaking underwater is it's like getting hit with a sledgehammer through a bag of potatoes. The whole force of it, but through the potatoes. When I came back up to the surface, I felt nothing, but then I looked to my left, just over my shoulder, and saw my leg floating in the other direction. It's at fucking eleven o'clock to where it ought to be. I'm thinking, 'This is weird – that leg's not supposed to be there.' And then, all of a sudden, the pain hits me. Oh my God, I've got quite a high pain threshold, but this has sailed way over it. All the people from the show are round me, trying to grab me out of the water, but every time they touch me, I'm like Chewbacca – 'Argh!' Now they've dragged me to the shore and they're trying to cut the fucking skis off. The cunts have given me the wrong fucking skis! They haven't given me the sock, which is supposed to detach.

Cut to the surgery – quite literally – and my fucking leg looks like an open kebab with two types of sauce: curry and ketchup. They've got the leg open, and I'm saying to the surgeons, 'Can you take pictures of this, because I need to go and speak to my lawyer about it . . . the wrong skis and all that?' They do the business, and it's settled out of court, and I ultimately end up getting compensated for everything. So that helped, but it wasn't worth the pain. The divorce was, though.

I remember my friend asking me, 'What's divorce like?' And I used that great old line, 'Well, it's kind of like getting your balls cut off through your wallet.' I always thought that was a great analogy – not through the front, but the leather holes in the back. When you open a wallet, there's usually a leather hole in the centre that goes down to the bottom, where sometimes a little penny will fall through. Squeeze your balls through that and then chop them off with a very sharp fucking cleaver. Not a razor; a meat cleaver, maybe. A rusty one. And there you kind of just about have it. It cost me well over half a million quid. God rest my ex-wife's soul . . . When I say that people usually ask, 'Is she not alive any more?' And then I say, 'Not to me she isn't.' Something about getting divorced seems to have brought out my inner Les Dawson.

Anyway, you go through what you go through, and then sometimes things work out in a way you couldn't have expected. Because out of what should've been, and was, one of the shittest times of my life – expensive divorce, big cocaine habit, leg fucked – came the best thing that's ever happened to me.

I had to cancel a gig in the Far East while I was in the hospital, and even when the rescheduled gig came around, I was still using crutches to get about. The date was 26 August 2006, and because my birthday was coming up three weeks later, there was a night in Shanghai which I was thinking of as a kind of advance birthday celebration. Little did I know I was about to receive the greatest gift of all, because my mate Dave Milligan was about to introduce me to my wife, Mika. I'll tell you how it happened, because it was really funny.

I'm at the dinner table with loads of people at the New Heights in Shanghai. It's a gorgeous place, on the main drag – lovely marble floors, really elegant, you can imagine some serious shit would've gone down there in the old days. It's kind of an art-deco vibe, but with a beautiful Eastern twist. Anyway, I'm sitting there when I get this phone call from Dave, who should've been there ages before. 'Fucking hell, Dave, where are you? This is meant to be our big night out.' His birthday's the day before mine, so it's kind of a joint celebration.

Anyway, he tells me he's not going to make it, but just as I'm processing that, this fucking bird walks in. Denim shorts. 'Fit' is not the word – even to use that terminology would be unworthy. 'Fucking beautiful' are the words. In fact, I've never seen a creature like her – she's got real natural style, and the sound of her heels as she walked across that marble floor . . .

'Hang on, Dave, you've got to wait, this fucking bird's just walked in.' 'I know,' he says. 'She's with me.' Then he pops his head through the door – he's made her take the lead! He's planned the whole thing. They come in and she sits down opposite me. I'm thinking, 'This fucking bird is one of his mates? If I had mates like that I wouldn't be wasting time with me. Wow!' I'm fascinated by her and just trying to think of anything I can do to keep the conversation going.

'So what do you do?' I ask, trying to act casual. That's a start, isn't it? She says something about 'helping people to get rid of clothes they don't want', which I don't quite catch, but there's something about her. I'm captivated. It turns out she's French-Canadian, and she's working for a company called Dynamite, or something like that, who have offices in Shanghai. It's not till later on I find out that she hates it. For the moment the evening's moving on. We all go out, play this set, it's amazing. And there's a geezer in the crowd who has this fucking brilliant t-shirt on. It's tan and ochre with the words 'Hi, you'll do' written on it in dark brown letters. I say to him, 'Mate, I'll swap you,' and give him whatever I'm wearing in return. Then I've got it on – I've still got this t-shirt more than ten years later, even though my dogs have tried to ravage it – and I'm looking at Mika across the dancefloor going, 'All right?' I'm laughing, but even as I'm laughing, I'm thinking, 'Hang on a minute, I might have a chance here.'

I think I'm temporarily off my crutches at that point. We're all having an amazing time, and even the fact that Mika – and this is something I'll never forget and she'll never live down – dances like Jimmy Somerville from Bronski Beat doesn't ruin the vibe. Who knew that a 'Smalltown Boy' was what I was looking for all along? That one certainly came out of left field.

So anyway, there's an after-party, and we all go back to the hotel, where everyone's getting head and hand massages. That's great – fantastic, nothing dubious, we're talking about worthy issues and everything else, I'm getting a head massage, fucking Mika's getting a head massage, and I'm thinking, 'This woman's got everything.' Of course, later on we end up doing something we always used to do for the craic if we had a hotel room, which is turn everything upside down: TV, bed, wall units, anything you can unscrew off the walls, just to be complete cunts so the cleaner gets freaked out. Anyway, we're busy doing that, and I'm about to leave – a bit the worse for wear, you won't be surprised to hear – so I call her over and lean in. I think, 'Just go for it' – the way you do when you're quite well refreshed – so I give her a kiss. Just one. Then I leave. Besotted. Absolutely fucking besotted.

A few days later, once I'm back in London, I'm ringing up Dave, first to apologise for the kiss, given that it was him she'd arrived with, then to say, 'Dave, I've got to talk to her, can you give me an email, anything?' So he does that, which is nice of him, and now I'm in touch with her, and I'm laying it on with a stick – 'I'm going to be in Japan, could we maybe meet up and talk about merchandise?' Because that's vaguely the field that she works in, and merchandise is the only thing that's on my mind at this point. Yeah, right. Anyway, I realise I'm going to have this kind of twin-bed set-up, and I convince her nothing untoward is going to happen. OK, cool. So she comes to fucking Japan, to stay in this hotel.

I'm bending over backwards to show what a gentleman I am – 'OK, do you want to freshen up or use the bathroom? That's cool. I'll go out. It's cool.' A friend of mine at the time – an Australian girl called Carla I've known for probably thirty-five years, from way back in Wolverhampton days; but she's a big player, had some business in Camden, went to raves, used to go out with the great boxer Sugar Ray Leonard – had given me this unbelievable piece of cinematography: a film called *Ashes and Snow* by a guy named Gregory Colbert. He's an installation photographer and a deep-sea diver and he went and lived with a tribe for years to shoot this film. You've got to see this piece to understand the level it's at. There are these women in it that kind of swirl, one of them ducks her head down and all of a sudden there's this fucking eagle . . . I realise this could sound like Enya, but it's the real shit.

Anyway, I'd seen this film and wanted to show it to Mika. There's a bit near the beginning where you see this guy diving and swimming around in the water and all these elephants are coming into the frame, then suddenly you see a monk with his eyes closed going backwards. That moment really took me back to a strange experience I'd had in the recording studio where we made the secret track 'The Dream Within', which was my suicide note backwards, but I'll tell you about that later.

In the meantime it was also strange that this film was narrated by a really good friend of mine, the actor Laurence Fishburne. 'Fish' – which is what me and Ozwald Boateng know him as, because those two have been tight for years – is the person who sat there at a party for Donatella Versace in this mad house once and just recited unbelievable poetry to the whole room. Afterwards I asked him, 'What the fuck was that?' And he explained that it was prison poetry from the thirties and forties. It was like early rap – beautiful stuff – then later he sent me the book. But I lent it to someone and they never gave it back. If you're reading this, whoever you are, you're a complete cunt. Not to spoil the romantic mood or anything.

Hearing Fish's familiar voice doing the voiceover on *Ashes and Snow* really made the words stick. Especially at the part of

ALL THINGS REMEMBERED

the film where he goes to the river and writes these love letters, then burns them and throws them in the water. So me and Mika were watching this film, sitting there with a box of tissues, just crying our eyes out. The way this experience planted an idea in my head, which I'll come back to later, was a bit like someone passing you the matchbox and going, '1634 Racine.' That's from the Kevin Costner gangster movie, *The Untouchables*. Robert De Niro's crying his eyes out in the opera, and then the murderer comes in and slips him the matchbox with Sean Connery's address on, so he can go and finish him off, and De Niro's like, 'Kill him, while I watch the opera.'

In the meantime I just turned to her and said, 'We're not going to fuck now, are we? It's not going to happen.' And we didn't. Instead we courted, which was the thing that really made me fall in love with her. I did the Hoffman and now I'd got courtship – for the first time in my life. I'd just cut the umbilical cord, and all the elastic bands had gone back to where they were going back to. I was free. She played me a fucking Beatles song I'd never heard – 'Real Love' – and I'm a Beatles fan. But 'Real Love' was new to me (though to be honest she could probably have played me 'Agadoo' at that stage and I'd have liked it). And I played her 'Once in a Lifetime' by Talking Heads; she'd never heard that. So we just played our favourite songs to each other with headphone splitters on bullet trains going around fucking Japan.

It was the combination of that experience and Larry's narration of the film that inspired me to write letters. So I bought lots of beautiful Japanese paper and I started writing letters to Mika, from above the clouds on planes, which I still do to this day. I've written hundreds and hundreds of them – if you saw them all together you'd think, 'Ooh, he's a bit warm, isn't he? He's a bit . . . *obsessed*' – and she never writes back, because she doesn't need to.

Mika doesn't say much, but when she does say something, it usually levels me – right back down to where I need to be. Whereas I'd go through these ridiculous letter-writing sessions. I sent one that was so small it needed to be read with a magnifying glass, but that was delivered inside a much bigger one. I sent one which was something like 10 foot by 8 foot in size. It was so big she had to unfold it in the living room – a huge letter written with a fucking massive pen. I'd also do lots of other obscure shit, like when I'd go and visit her I'd leave a letter somewhere and tell her, 'Under the box in the red thing on the stairs there's a letter for you.' By that time my spell had been cast – or the Stockholm syndrome had well and truly kicked in, whichever way you want to look at it – so she would always go and find them. I'd also send her off-the-wall intergalactic videos with *Star Wars* backing-track music, so she knew I was mad from the beginning.

She must've been OK with that, though, because about four months into our courtship, I went back to Shanghai to see her, thinking, 'Well, we're kind of dating now, aren't we? We really officially are . . . fuck! We haven't done it yet! Let's get it out the fucking way . . .' So we got all that shit out the way very quickly – extremely quickly! And more than ten years later we're still married and we're bringing up our daughter Koko together. Mika's the muse of my universe. She's real, but she's also unreal. And of course none of these happy circumstances would've unfolded if I hadn't had the accident so that the gig was cancelled and I could go back later and meet her. So that's why I call it 'the Beautiful Accident'.

C2. Monkey Boots, Tomatoes and Goldfish Obstetrics

Part of the healing process of writing those endless letters to Mika was being able to see, through some of the stories I told her, that not all of my memories of childhood were bad. There had also been some moments that were really beautiful, or at least had beautiful elements, in which I could see the ways in which I'd tried to make the best of the childhood that I'd had. For example, running down the street in monkey boots when they're new . . . as anyone who's done it as a child will tell you, you're the fastest kid on the block – I mean, insanely fast, like something in a comic book. Especially when the rubber ankle protectors give you superhuman powers and you're wearing your short denim cut-offs and the Fireball Gang t-shirt you'd bought with a postal order the week before.

The tomatoes story was also about being – or at least feeling – superhuman. It's obvious why a kid who doesn't have much control over their circumstances would find solace in this fantasy. But the excitement I felt when I opened the door of the forbidden greenhouse and stepped inside went far beyond make-believe. The only way I can capture the feeling of closing that door behind me – the sense of a vacuum sealing me in and the deadly silence of heat – was by referring to David Bowie's 'Space Oddity' – 'Here am I floating in a tin can . . .'. It was so inconceivable I might as well have been in outer space.

The reason that greenhouse was such uncharted territory was because it was my foster-mother's husband's pride and joy – his fucking throne room. This was Fred, the guy who as far as I was concerned didn't seem to do much apart from watch the wrestling and beat the fuck out of me. Outside the house there was a fence, then an allotment, then this greenhouse, and obviously the idea of me ever going into it was completely unthinkable. But somehow there I was, inside, looking at these tomatoes – the tall green plants stretching up towards the glass panels – and taking another step forward with these fucking monkey boots on. The crisp sound of a leaf disintegrating under my foot on the tiled mosaic floor was like a flame igniting.

I reached my left hand up above my head to cup one of the massive, juicy tomatoes, gently taking the weight off it to get some idea of how heavy these beauties were. They were so shiny I could see my face in them. All of a sudden I could take in the whole reality of those giant fruits and their lush leaves and the lime-green stalks and the pungent smell of vinegar – lemon almost. And that's when I noticed the flies drifting lazily through the torrid afternoon like punctuation marks, gathering to make sense of the letter I would one day write to Mika about them.

And then I realised I was a fucking ninja, and I knew I could catch those flies in the air and kill them; in fact, I could actually be such a ninja that I could catch one and release it and then even fly like it myself. I'd become super-fast. Somehow as I whirled about the greenhouse either dispatching flies or gently redirecting them according to my divine whim, some – well, maybe quite a lot – of those ripe tomatoes got dislodged from their stalks and squashed beneath my new boots.

Then, just as I was looking at my reflection in the shiny tomato skins on the floor, I saw a different kind of mirror image – the furious, contorted face of a very angry tomato indeed. Of course this vengeful apparition was none other than Fred, the master of the greenhouse himself, who reached into his desecrated sanctuary, dragged me out of there, and duly beat the fuck out of me.

ALL THINGS REMEMBERED

After the beating and being sent to my room, the dream of superhuman ninja monkey-boot powers was just a bubble that had burst, especially once I learned in a biology lesson a few months later that the only reason I could catch the flies so easily was because they had become drowsy and docile from prolonged exposure to the greenhouse's intense heat. Luckily, that didn't happen to me.

I realise that from the perspective of someone who wasn't there it might be hard to see what is beautiful or even vaguely positive about this story. But that's the parallax of memory, isn't it? For me the sense of possibility and excitement I got from being inside that greenhouse was more exceptional than the beating that came afterwards, so that was the part that really stayed with me.

Before the gate that led to the greenhouse, there was another gate in a picket fence around a figure-of-eight pond which had some goldfish in it. One morning I woke up and realised that one of Fred's goldfish was pregnant. I knew I needed to save the fish because the pregnancy was taking too long and the poor girl was suffering – she was starting to swim on her side because she was so full. So I decided to try and help by getting her out of the pond and giving her a little squeeze. Basically, my good intentions came to nothing, as I ended up squeezing the internals out of this fucking fish that was already on its way out. Of course Fred caught me red-handed – or gold-handed – bursting his fish in his fucking pool.

That was another beating, and I can see how it didn't look too good from his point of view – 'The little fucker is killing my fish now!' There was no margin in me trying to explain that I was only trying to help. I don't think I was conscious enough of the idea of explaining something to even try. And he wouldn't have listened even if I had.

C3. A Molten State

The central importance of art in my life isn't just about the music or the films or the paintings I put my name to. It goes deeper than that. Art is the well from which I draw the resources to help me face pretty much every challenge that life throws at me.

For example, if I have to make a speech in public, then in order for me to relax in the presence of a crowd of people, I have to visualise the experience as though I were standing before a very large canvas, preparing to apply my lines and thoughts freely to the gathering. Otherwise there's a real risk I'll just end up standing looking at everyone strangely for fifteen minutes. But if I close my eyes and conceptualise, I can go to the moon – I arrive, I imagine, I come back. Then when I open my eyes I've just got to physically work out the fuel I need to get there, and how I'm going to build the rocket.

I learned early on that if you can't say it, spray it. It's like the critic Joseph Rykwert said: 'What makes an artist is the application of a medium to the surface' – whether that be paint coming out of an aerosol can, sound coming out of the needle on a dubplate, an MC spitting lyrics through a microphone, or a breakdancer defying gravity on a piece of lino. It doesn't matter what the name on the paintbox is – music, graffiti, jewellery, sculpture, acting – the colours are still the same.

I can see that on one level this is a child-like way to approach the world, and you could argue that my attachment to art has allowed at least a part of me to never grow up. But at the same time it's also been the means by which my character has developed. And as with any evolution there is a factor of time: time for

68   ALL THINGS REMEMBERED

thoughts to mature in one's mind, and time for feelings to mature in one's heart.

Over the past three and a half decades I have been blessed to experience so much creativity and artistry in my life – from making murals in Wolverhampton to bombing trains with my heroes in New York; from casting jewellery in Miami to sand-blasting tree trunks in Hertfordshire; from writing, producing and performing music to acting in films and appearing in documentaries and on reality TV. Yet however different the various projects I've been involved with might appear from the outside, the impulse that drives everything I do is fundamentally the same.

It all goes back to an extremely vivid memory from when I was making gold teeth at the flea market in Miami. I was watching some gold melt, and seeing this precious metal move and change shape under the impact of the heat made me realise something very important.

When you melt the gold to make grills, what darts across the surface is like chrome – totally different to the actual colour of the metal when it's solid. The impact of the oxygen-acetylene is almost a white-out – the molten gold becomes this magical blue-tinted white, and the silver on the surface is as clear as liquid, but it darts around in a totally chaotic way. That's my life right there – the chaos – but within that chaos there is something that makes sense, and if you concentrate hard enough, the patterns will surely become clear . . .

Knowing I could change the structure of something precious that was seemingly so solid and unchangeable led me to believe that I might also have the power to melt some of the hardened feelings inside myself, which had fused and melded together in the crucible of the darker times of my childhood, and maybe reshape them into something more positive. The awareness stirred inside me that I had the power to shape the world around me for the better.

It was centrifugal casting that taught me this. It was so beautiful to see the hot silver darting across the surface in chaos, hitting the hammer, spinning it into the mould, taking it into the crucible, seeing the gold shoot into the mould, taking it apart, putting it into the water, the hot steam breaking apart, and there's my piece of gold. I've changed the form.

Maybe this all sounds a bit abstract, so I'd like to zoom in on the guy who taught me to do it, and how he and I came to be in the same place at the same time. I've been lucky enough to have a series of great mentors in my life, and Orlando Plein was Miami's finest. He was one of a family of five brothers who originally came from Surinam, and his older brother Eddie was the guy who pretty much single-handedly invented the culture of gold teeth – at least as it's understood in hip-hop culture.

Forget all the new breed you hear about from Atlanta and

elsewhere in the American South, Eddie was basically the one who started it all. He set up a shop called Eddie's Golds at the Colosseum in Brooklyn, New York City, and while he was there he made gold teeth for pretty much a rapper's Who's Who – Just-Ice, Ice-T, Flavor Flav of Public Enemy, Jay-Z when he was seventeen.

His brother Orlando learned the craft – and it is a craft, as I'll explain in a minute – and came down to Miami to set up a booth at Flea Market USA number 1. I was out in Miami in search of my dad at the time. I'd tried to get into the whole beach thing and the art-deco thing: I'd gone out fishing for marlin with these two Jewish brothers called Bernie and Mats, but none of it really felt like me. Then I went down to the Flea Market and it was just totally gangsta. I knew that was where I belonged, and when I came across Orlando in this booth called New York Connection (which was something that we both had when I think about it now) I showed him my portfolio with some of my graffiti and my airbrushing, and he just said, 'Let's get you set up.'

We shared the rent for the booth and at first I airbrushed t-shirts and painted drug dealers' cars while he did the golds, but pretty soon he started to teach me centrifugal casting – which he still does in that place to this day, using the same machine as when I was there. He passed on a lot of important background knowledge – like the fact that you can't put iron in your mouth, because the golds will go green, so it has to be 24 carat or 18 carat with zinc, and you should only get it from a dental supplier, not from a jeweller – and then he introduced me to a process that still fascinates me now. I owe a lot to him in terms of him showing me mad game.

What I loved about making gold teeth was the complexity of the craft. When you get them from a dentist they'll just take a print of your jaw and send it off to another lab. The set of skills Orlando taught me had nothing in common with either that or the Ratner's way of doing things or the shitty 'one size fits all' gold teeth you can get online now. That kind of shoddy practice is the bane of the true craftsman.

There are so many stages to doing it properly: taking the moulds, waxing up the teeth on the moulds, waxing up the design, layering the whole thing up so you have enough bed for the diamonds to sit on, crafting it by hand, setting it up on sprues, putting the gold onto a ball in the investment cement, taking it out and putting it into an oven, then casting it with a centrifugal cast, then breaking it out of there and sawing the fucking sprues off so you've got these basic gold teeth. Then you get the drill and sand them out before putting them back on the moulds, finely finishing them, and polishing them to the design. Then you get the diamonds and the stones set inside those fucking teeth and that is it – all done in a week.

From the point Orlando taught me this process, it was almost like I was no longer alone – as if the things that were outside me and the person within could somehow work together. That collaboration has not always been an easy one, and in hard times I go back to that moment time and again, trying to ensure I can keep the part of me I discovered that day alive, reminding myself that my mind has to allow itself to be fluid for my feelings and ideas to be in motion.

This image is not just a verbalisation of what I do, it's the life-blood of my existence. To be in a molten state is my best hope of adapting to a constantly accelerating world. For me the struggle, the effort has always been to reconcile what's inside of me, and what I see around me, to the medium at hand, always adapting and evolving.

Over the years I've worked on endless numbers of different projects in many different areas of creative expression – often with the same themes reoccurring, weaving in and out;

sometimes switching the medium but applying the same technique; trying to approach completion and closure and each time getting a little closer to closing my circle, while at the same time knowing that this circle can never be closed and this process is the cycle that propels us through our lives. The lessons I learned from my acting mentor Clint Dyer are the perfect example. After I'd played his nemesis in a gangster movie with David Bowie, he cast me in the play *Kingston 14* at Stratford East, and through that live theatre experience got things out of me as an actor that no one else had ever done.

Like the incomplete circle, men and women cannot help feeling somewhat hand-drawn themselves: imperfect, incomplete and never still. I know that the life I describe in these pages will seem quite chaotic and out of control to a lot of people. It often seems that way to me. But I've been lucky to know that whenever I feel imperfect or incomplete – which is pretty much all the time, obviously – art of one kind or another will be there to show me the way forward. It's the still centre and the driving force at the same time.

You know that thing when you're sat down at a dinner table with someone famous and you've had a few drinks so you ask them the question no one would usually dare to? That happened to me with the Labour politician Ed Balls. I leant over to him and asked, 'Why do you like politics? Level with me, just between me and you . . .' He leant back over to me and said, 'Power.' And when he said that, I thought, 'That's what it is, right there. There's the devil I know.' On the one hand, I knew he was just telling me that to get me off his back, but on the other I respected him for telling me the fucking truth.

That's the kind of conversation I can imagine myself having with some of these drum 'n' bass gentrifying bastards who think it's a good idea to work with Gary Barlow. It'd start off the same way: 'Come on, tell me the truth, man, you know it's bollocks, right? You know what you're doing is bollocks. Just between you and I, admit to me now that it's bollocks.'

'Yeah, yeah, it's bollocks.'

'OK, that's great. Finally you admit it after giving me the runaround. You admit that it's bollocks. There you go, then. It almost infuriates me even more that you're only now telling the truth, but at least you are finally doing it. Because now at least we can both agree that as far as drum 'n' bass is concerned, you no longer have any stake in the matter. No credibility, zero anything, because that is not what we do. Don't pretend it is, and that's the end of it.

'To me, certain things are out of bounds. This genre is so beautiful, and earns us money, and I get the fact there's a certain greed and a certain jealousy that you weren't quite the Robin Hoods that we were. And I realise that you don't understand that. But listen, even me and Robbie Williams in the nineties – doing really good Peruvian Flake together at four in the morning – knew that us making a record together was going to be a bad idea. And if anyone from Take That was going to have something to do with drum 'n' bass, Robbie Williams, just for the record, went to Blue Note. Robbie Williams, for the record, liked the music. Robbie Williams, for the record, realised that him making a drum 'n' bass track was not going to be the thing to do.

'But Gary fucking Barlow? I wish you all the best. I hope you get another number one, a new extension, a new car, even a new girlfriend. But you don't have a fucking say, sunshine, because when you signed that cheque, we cut the fucking corner off it. It is null and void. It's very simple: you don't have a say, so shut up. Meet me on a plane, wave to me, say, "Hello, how's it going?" but do not talk to me about drum 'n' bass music.'

The funny thing that happens is that we do actually end up having this conversation – it steps out of the realm of hypothesis and becomes a fact – because this kid calls me 'to clear something up'. Well, now Pandora's box is open, because he's phoned me, so whatever the reason he decided that was a good idea, he's going to have to listen to me now.

I said to him, 'Listen, kid, you know, you're really annoying me now, but let me just break it down for you . . . when you're having a shit tonight' – and he started laughing: 'What do you mean? What do you mean?' that's what he says, so I carry on – 'When you're having a shit tonight, and your shit's at its widest girth and your eyes are watering, think to yourself, when you think about your musical fucking heroes, do you go fucking "Gary Barlow, Paloma Faith"? No, you don't, before it plops into the fucking abyss. No, you don't.'

It's like the old saying, 'Let sleeping dogs lie' . . . but don't call sleeping dogs on a Sunday and ask them to 'clear something up'. Just to break this down so you understand what happened, this guy had called me because GQ, who has been in this scene from its very humble beginnings and is a respected OG who is entitled to his opinion, had responded to his Tweet about whatever power-pop bullshit he was doing – because that's what it is, it's power pop, it ain't drum 'n' bass – with a very simple reply: 'Gary Barlow, drum 'n' bass, no thank you.'

Now to me, that's totally fair enough, because if you put something out there in public, then other people are entitled to respond to it – but that does not equate to sending personal texts to people's phones. Because if you're so convinced that '80,000 teenage fans can't be wrong', why should you give a shit what two old cronies like me and GQ have to say about it?

How dare you think that whatever you do represents what my fucking music is about? Or what any of this scene is? And don't come at me with Justin Bieber – all that drum 'n' Bieber bollocks – because at least he owns it. He's a great singer and a great songwriter. Not like you, pretending to be a pop star with your fucking dodgy sunglasses, German haircut and new leather jacket, hiding behind this thing which maybe glances drum 'n' bass but could never in a million fucking years fucking be it. Maybe you didn't feel you were getting the fame because you missed that really big wave. I get it. You can do what you want – no one's telling you that you can't. Just don't do it in my face, or I'll shut you down before you can say 'Relight my fire'.

Because the difference between you and Andy C is that Andy still has the decency to play a fucking tune when I'm standing next to him in a club. And the difference between you and DJ Fresh is that at least DJ Fresh came along with someone that was unknown – like Rita Ora was when they did 'Hot Right Now' together – and made a fucking good tune, because that's the great producer that he is. This didn't even come up in the conversation, but if you think about Future Cut, Darren and Tunde, they got it right. They made some great drum 'n' bass tracks, and then they fucked off to LA and produced some great tunes for Tom Jones. But is there a place for drum 'n' bass on a Tom Jones record? No, there isn't.

Don't try to tell me that this is 'subjective'. Subjective is three adults having a conversation, not the Coachman and Lampwick taking Pinocchio to the funfair. So keep me out of your circus, you clowns – I ain't got no time for it. And as for the accusation that what GQ said was 'racist', well, I'm with GQ on that one – 'If you think my comment regarding Gary Barlow was racist, then you're a bigger cunt than I thought you were.'

It's crazy how power forgets the people who laid the table for it in the first place. Of course, that's no less true of Ed Balls as he chows down on his steak at my expense, but at least he has the decency to be honest about his motivation, and at least he's eating steak, not serving McDonald's Happy Meals to the kids on plates that we paid for.

I've always been misunderstood as far as race is concerned. Growing up in children's homes in Wolverhampton and Walsall, being moved around a lot, I would obviously get called things. My first nickname at school was 'Paki'. Can you fucking believe that one? But that's what they called me, and I accepted it.

One part of the reason I did was because I didn't want to get beaten to death by loads of white kids, but the other part was that I didn't really understand the real meaning of the word. Obviously what it meant in the most basic sense was, 'You look like a Pakistani.' And I guess I did, in a sense. My skin was light, but it wasn't white. And when it came to the nuances of that, no one was there to explain anything for me. All I had to learn from was the things people said and did to me.

I had a really awful music teacher at school. Not only was she completely ruthless, she also played the piano really badly. But no one could tell her when she played those off-notes, even though we all felt like cringing. Even as kids with no musical knowledge, we knew it was out of tune. She had this song she used to try to play – a sea shanty called 'The Dark Mulatto'. I didn't find out what that word meant till later, when I was told that it meant 'half-caste'.

Now that is apparently not politically correct – 'mixed race' is supposed to be the right way of saying it. But for me, when you think about being half from one caste and half from another, it kind of makes sense. I don't see anything wrong with that, to be honest. I certainly don't find it offensive, in the same way I don't mind calling my boys from Miami my niggers – because they're

my niggers from Miami, in the same way that my niggers from New York are my niggers from New York, because that's what it is. It's when a white person says it that it becomes something really bad, apparently, so there you go. Not always, but sometimes. You can hear it in the tone.

I suppose the first cultural thing I really got involved in was punk. I was just a kid – maybe two or three years too young to really get into it, but I loved The Stranglers. Obviously what punk was predominantly driven by was white anger. If you think about the unions at that time, and all the strikes they were calling, leading to Scargill and the miners revolting against Thatcher a bit later on, white people were getting very uppity all of a sudden.

But there were black people too, alongside them, in the same way that there are white people in the ghetto who have listened to black music for a long time. Just because they're white, does that mean music of black origin can't rub off on them in the right way? The same way The Stranglers rubbed off on me. And what is the right way anyway? If someone really understands that music and loves it to a certain degree, I think we're all entitled to that. We shouldn't make it elitist (except where Gary Barlow's concerned), even though it's that very generosity of spirit which opens the door to gentrification – of music poor people love, as well as of the places where they live.

From my own point of view, being called 'Paki' in school obviously made me ask questions about my own identity. 'Who are my parents? Well, my dad is black and my mum is Scottish.' That was a real 'wow' moment for me. It seems ridiculous now, but it took me a long time to realise what my parental situation actually meant. In my children's home, there was one black guy – ironically named Trevor White – and that was it. Apart from the white girl who tried to speak Jamaican because she was seeing a black guy – I think he worked at Whispering Wheels – and was years ahead of her time, because in a few years every white kid in the suburbs would be doing that.

Back in the seventies, black culture was still more of a closed shop, especially growing up in an environment that was more or less all white. The only way I would begin to understand that side of me was through Steel Pulse being a British reggae band, and lovers rock and Bob Marley and all of that. But if that was the positive side of being half black, the negative side was harder to get away from.

It wasn't just about getting bullied at school, though I'd always get cornered in what was meant to be my educational environment. There were definitely streets I couldn't walk down because I knew I'd get fucking beaten up. Kids from the year above always wanted to fight me when they saw me out and about. 'All right, Paki?' would start out sounding friendly, almost like a term of endearment, but then it would turn into, 'Oi, you, Paki!' The phonetics of it became aggressive, and then you knew a kicking was on its way.

I think England was very much like South Africa in those days. Mixed-race people, or people of two origins – 'the coloureds', as they'd call us – are often looked down on from both black and white sides, which is quite strange. At that point you were either 'Blackie' or 'Chalky' or like me – in that middle place which no one really understood.

As a consequence of this, it took me years to work out who I really was. By the time I was thinking, 'Hang on a minute, I don't want to be called "Paki" any more,' I had more or less left school. Apart from Trevor White, the only other black guy I'd really had experience of being around was another kid called Trevor, who gets a mention in my poem about Hammerwich. He was darker-skinned than me, and had an afro – you know, massive hair – which I couldn't manage. My hair was kind of curly, but the curls were tight. Being different to everyone else seemed to mean that people would constantly go out of their way to alienate you, or at least do little things to make clear that you weren't one of the group.

I don't know to what extent this shaped my character, or whether to a certain degree I was a loner anyway. But the one thing I always seemed to be able to connect through was the music – even though that took me to some unlikely places. Going back to when the skinhead and punk movements were around, in the late seventies and early eighties, you'd see me wearing a donkey jacket, tight jeans and eighteen-hole Dr Martens. I'd go over to the youth club on the Manor Farm estate. That was where I'd meet up with this guy called Ray and his brother, who were really fucking racist, and they'd force me to do glue with them over by the canal, so I'd go back to the children's home practically delirious and frothing at the mouth, thinking, 'What the fuck's going on?'

It wasn't so much a trend, it was more a kind of culture thing that you'd get into – well, I would, anyway. Then when they'd put music on at the youth club, you'd quickly realise that when they started moshing with each other – throwing each other around – you were the one who was going to get the worst of it. That's when it really starts coming out in those white people, when there's a situation where someone is going to get a kicking, and there's a kid who isn't quite white there. So when Public Image Limited or GBH or the Sex Pistols would go on the record player it always tended to be me that got a kicking. And you'd kind of get up and brush yourself off and try to think, 'Yeah – I'm one of the boys.'

That kind of racism did not go away. When I was at the Frank F. Harrison School, near Walsall, the Beechdale estate which was next to it was infamous for its connections to the National Front. By that time, there was a black guy called Eric Smith who was in my class. He ended up going into the army, which you could understand as a consequence of just wanting to be somebody and do whatever. I've got back in touch with Eric over the last few years, which is interesting, because he ended up becoming a teacher. Anyway, him, David Warner and a girl called Heather Campbell were the black kids in the class. I was the lone mixed-race kid, and then there was a guy called Whitehead, who was white but his mum was seeing a black guy, so he could speak patois more fluently than anyone, and in a kind of self-conscious way was more black than the black kids in the class. He was the one I smoked my first spliff with, to UB40's 'King', in our school dinner break.

He rolls this fucking spliff, and I'm like, 'What the fuck's weed, man, what's it do?' He tells me, 'This is going to fucking sort you out, this is.' And I smoked this spliff. I remember leaning on his mum's sofa and all of a sudden I thought it was the end of the world. I fell and fell and fell and fell, and then – bang – he put this record on the gramophone and it was 'King' – 'Where are your people now?' And I was just, like, 'What the fuck is this? Where *are* my people now?' It blew my mind.

Whitehead had black people around him too, like Joy Regan, who was actually a mixed-race girl. She had an afro and she was fucking beautiful, but she always had these panda rings around her eyes, like she'd been crying for fucking years. I did fancy her, I guess partly because she looked more like me than anyone else did, but she only went out with white guys.

My first mixed-race girlfriend was at a holiday camp – maybe Butlin's in Minehead, or somewhere. I snogged her and then she gave me her phone number and I waved goodbye to her on the coach. Later on I called her with 2p from a phone box, but I don't think we ever spoke again after that.

Just occasionally, it can be brilliant being mixed race – when you get the best of both worlds. I'm both a Member of the British Empire and a Massive Bell-End. I look at black, I look at white, I'm on the fence, but that doesn't mean I'm not proud to be British: I grew up on fucking Steel Pulse and Slade, mate – tell me about it. It can also be a total pain in the arse, though, when you feel like you don't belong anywhere and you're just having to take shit from everybody.

I remember Eric and the others asking, 'Why are they calling you "Paki", man?' But then they'd call me it, too – it was just one of those things and a sign of how alienated I was from actually being black. Heather Campbell would often jibe me, 'You're not really black – you're half black, but you're more white,' so I'd always have that as well. It was really confusing as a kid, but I'd just try to roll with the punches and keep coming back for more.

It's interesting to look back and see how those attitudes were echoed in the music industry at that time, but maybe in a more subtle way. There's a documentary about that great man Jazzie B and the impact Soul II Soul had on the world called *From Dole to Soul,* where Tony Hadley from Spandau Ballet is talking about all those British bands like Imagination and Beggar & Co. who came through in the early eighties with music that was very influenced by American funk artists. Now before that Hadley had been doing all this new romantic stuff, but then he got inspired by all this black funk that was coming along, and that didn't go too badly for Spandau Ballet, did it? On that documentary you see them on tour with Beggar & Co., who were a really good band in their own right, but suddenly they're playing second fiddle – or more precisely, second horn section – to Tony Hadley, who, by his own admission, was basically saying, 'All of a sudden it's white, and people get it.'

I wouldn't hold that against him on any level – it's honest of him to admit it. What's weirder is the way some white people look at black culture: the way they get so much from it and yet are very quick to deny that and will be really racist when they get the chance. Like the ones who'll say, 'Yeah, I don't mind black people, I've got a baseball cap and trainers . . .' That's never going anywhere good.

It took me a long time to really get my head around how all this stuff worked. But once I came out of school people soon stopped calling me 'Paki', and my nickname became 'Disco' when I was going roller-skating, because I used to like disco music and I wore these moon boots that had a kind of disco look to them. At that stage in my life I really gravitated towards black people, like Granty, this black guy I knew who used to drive a three-litre Capri. And my brother, Melvin, who I felt a real connection with when I left the children's home and started living with him and my mother for a while.

When I first turned up at my mum's house and met Melvin there, his missus at the time – Annette – was pregnant. I could

ALL THINGS REMEMBERED

smell weed all through the house. And my mum met me on the balcony: 'Come in and have a cup of tea, your brother's upstairs.' I hadn't seen Melvin for a couple of years. I went upstairs, and he was there in the bed, with this fucking weed, and his missus was pregnant, but he had loads of Rasta pictures on the wall – Selassie, lion, Pablo Gad, all these pictures – I'll never forget it.

My family were up to stuff at that time. We used to break into a lot of factories. My brother was the one, you know: a right piece of work and not to be messed with. Melvin's younger than me, but he was always kind of older in his head because he was very street – fucking mad as a box of frogs as well. If you think I'm out there, you should meet Melvin. Anyway, our main partners in crime were these two brothers who lived over the main bridge. I think they'd met my brother at blues dances, probably the Half Moon or somewhere like that, and they were really tall – and they were Rastas too. But they were fucking naughty.

At that point, because my brother had locks and everyone else had locks – 'Ah, you fucking baldhead, you should have locks' – becoming a Rasta seemed like the natural thing to do to fit in. I think I was eighteen or nineteen at the time. So I was doing that, waxing up my hair, which was fucking painful. Beeswax. You've got to get your hair, wash it in salt water, pull the hair into a clump, then pull it down until it kind of makes just a knot, and then you beeswax it from the root all the way up, and you roll it back, and you leave it in a hat for fucking two months like that. And then you just basically wash it all out. It kind of falls out, in a crusty way. Some parts are really hard and stay with the wax inside them, but then when it finally leaves your hair, you basically have this Aero bar kind of fucking mess.

I didn't dye it, but I was always washing it with salt, so in the summer it would get really light at the top and round the edges.

That was how I started to get called 'Goldie Locks' – 'cos even though I was doing this thing that was thought of as very black, my hair was still very, very light. On the one hand it was good to have that black identity to tap into, because as a kid I was always trying to find my place. But on the other I never felt like I fully belonged there.

Trying to be a Rasta in the inner city is very, very difficult, because it's more of a rural thing, and there's no way you can go and live in the woods when you're in Wolverhampton. Also, you're doing all these things which are almost like religious observance – like waxing up your hair and staying away from any food that contains animal fat – and yet it's still OK to rob some old dear's bag when she's going to bingo on a Saturday night so you've got money to buy weed. How ironic and fucked up is that?

I think because I gravitated so strongly towards black culture, while still feeling that I came from slightly outside it, I always loved the music that got made when white people tried to adapt black music to work for them. I have already mentioned Spandau Ballet, but at that point – in the early eighties – pop music was full of people trying to do that: from Heaven 17, who were coming out of electronic music into something which was more affiliated to soul and funk, which I really loved, to Pigbag from Bristol, to Paul Weller moving on from The Jam to try to put a clearer streak of funk into what he was doing with The Style Council, even if his old fans didn't necessarily like it too much.

I loved all that stuff at the time and, even going back to older music from the sixties and seventies, I was drawn to white music which was very open and explicit about its black influence. Much as I loved The Beatles – and God bless you, George Harrison, for finding yourself when you started playing the sitar and went to India to hang out with the Maharishi – I really liked the way The Rolling Stones always put rhythm and blues first and foremost. Mick Jagger would always be saying, 'Hey, man, the blues, man, Bo Diddley, man,' and that was what I grew up on culturally – the blues aspect of 'Angie'.

So I was always drawn to black music that was being adapted by white people because somewhere in between the two was a place where I kind of fitted in. Then, by the time I was going roller-skating at Whispering Wheels, I was plugging into all this black music that gave me much more of a sense of belonging. That would give me the chemical constituents in my brain for hip-hop culture to really blow up for me a few years later. That was a musical environment where you didn't necessarily have to be black, because there were all these other different elements in it – Cuban, Colombian, Brazilian – which amalgamated into something that was very diverse but very unified at the same time.

Graffiti was the thing which really translated it all into three dimensions for me. Because this was a subculture which didn't belong to any particular colour. You had all these different writers – white, black, Hispanic – all gravitating towards the one hieroglyphic, the graffito, this shared visual, physical language that all the people from below the breadline had in common.

Coming from the care system as I did – foster homes, children's homes – I obviously felt a very strong need to be a part of a family. Looking at trains and thinking, 'These kids are writing their names from one end of the city to the other,' I finally felt like I'd found one. That was really, really important for me, to feel a part of that culture, especially with the mixed-race thing as well.

No one in New York would ever see a painted subway train and say, 'Oh, look at that Hispanic train going by' – or 'that Puerto Rican train' or 'that Afro-American train'. There were just all these kids that were doing their hieroglyphics that were very difficult for the outside world to understand, but we understood them: that's the point of the Wildstyle. That's why you don't just do retarded bubble letters for the rest of fucking society to read: why should I have to spell it out if I don't want to?

These were the smoke signals from the Bronx and the other boroughs, billowing out to the surrounding tribes. That's also how drum 'n' bass music would be, a few years later – it came from these inner cities in the UK that weren't just black, they were white and mixed race as well, and all the different musical genres from before fed into it; it was like the roughage that was left over. The reason I chose the name Rufige Kru to release some of my first records under was because that was how I thought you spelt the word 'roughage'! (Though I knew that wasn't how you were meant to spell 'crew'.)

C6. Pat Metheny and Frank Frazetta –
the Big Guys . . .

All good music has to take from the past to move forward. I look at Sun Ra, I look at the Stones and 'Angie', I look at Pat Metheny, who's been one of the biggest inspirations in my entire life . . . When I got an email from him telling me that the version of his 'Are You Going with Me?' which I've done on *The Journey Man* 'did a beautiful thing with the piece', that's one of the proudest moments I've had in music. That song is definitely one of my favourite records of all time, and it's been in my life for more than a quarter of a century.

The first time I heard 'Are You Going with Me?' I was sat in my dad's front room in Miami. I'd gone down there to get to know him and met this kind of stranger who looked like me. He was living in a house in Carol City, where I'd get up in the middle of the night and listen to Jazz FM on a tower stack system, like an Amstrad. I heard it a few times, in fact, because they'd play a load of tracks in a row without talking in between, and I kept missing the announcement as to what song it was. Finally, one night I heard, 'That was Pat Metheny – "Are You Going with Me?"' and so I went and found the record it came from, which was The Pat Metheny Group's third album, *Offramp*.

I wasn't so sure about the rest of the album, apart from 'Au Lait', which grew on me. It was their later album, *Still Life (Talking)*, which taught me everything I know about arrangement – how to introduce a motif with a solo and reinvent it further down the line with another instrument. I still think that's his greatest album. It's a beautiful canvas of life, and that's why I put the song 'Still Life' on *Timeless*, as a tribute.

Anyway, while I was in Miami, I'd be working the flea markets from Thursday to Saturday, doing gold teeth and spray-painting t-shirts. Then on a Sunday me and Orlando Plein would break out and go to Bayside and get crazy drunk on strawberry and pine-apple daiquiris. It wasn't really happening for me at my dad's, so after a while I moved in with Orlando and Cheryl, his girlfriend at the time, at his auntie's house on 177th Street. There were orange trees in the back garden, so we'd live on orange juice and this Surinamese chicken dish Cheryl would make called Brena Bona. She'd cook a big dish of it up on Saturday and it would probably last till the next Thursday. I was on a very steep learning curve in Miami – and not just when it came to cook-ing. All the Puerto Rican gangsters would talk to me in Spanish because they thought I looked Latin. All this comes back to me when I hear *Still Life (Talking)* – along with the experience of painting drug-dealers' cars. They'd come round to the booth to get a couple of t-shirts or some gold teeth. Deals would be done – cough, cough, hint, hint – and I'd suddenly find myself air-brushing the sides of some quite heavy people's low-riders and Nissan Pathfinders.

This wasn't a situation in which making a mistake would've been a good idea. This one guy asked me to airbrush a picture of him with his Uzi and his MAC – I didn't know what the latter looked like until he pulled his sub-machine gun out and showed it to me. 'Is that an Uzi in your pocket or are you just pleased to see me?' That was the kind of joke no one would really be making.

They probably didn't know these were the first times I'd ever done that job, but it wasn't so different to doing the t-shirts. It's basically the same process – getting the car paint, working out how much thinner to use to facilitate the application of the medium to the surface. All you've got to do is flatten down the sides and the hood of the vehicle – sand them down to a nice finish – then you get the image, get a top-feed airbrush, work out the consistency and airbrush the image with the colours. Then you send it to the car shop and they lacquer it. I'd do the hood and the side panels, from the door to the back. It would always be done freehand. Working on a truck the pieces will be smaller and more refined than they would be on a wall, and you've got to layer the detail differently, but there's a certain amount of freedom. It's just a question of adapting to the new environment.

It was the same thing when we went on road trips to do gold teeth in Nashville and Jacksonville, where we worked out of a snakeskin-suit shop. I did a mural on the wall of a guy called Johnny's two-door Jaguar XJS coupé I was pretty pleased with. I was learning how to make jewellery at this time, too, because if you can make gold teeth you can make a ring: it's just a question of taking what you've learned in the micro aspect and blowing it up within the same basic process.

Gold teeth, bam! Jewellery, bam! T-shirts, bam! Cars, bam! It's the same principle, you've just got to zoom in and out. Make it big, make it small, whatever the medium requires. I would never do letter-form when I was painting – it always came down to more character-based stuff – almost comic-booky in a way. The guy whose work I was always referring to was Frank Frazetta, even though he was an artist who painted in oils, rather than the Boris type of airbrushing. Look him up! If you look at the original *Conan the Barbarian* paperbacks, that's Frank Frazetta. Him, Metheny, those were the big guys for me . . .

SIDE D

D1. 'The Logical Song', or How Music Became the Timeline

There are two very cinematic episodes in my childhood which I've always associated with the songs that soundtrack them in my mind. The first was at Hammerwich children's home, between Chasewater and the Brownhills. As my earlier poem will have made clear, that was a scary place to be – very Dickensian, with a huge sweeping staircase, and haunted like fuck. You heard very bad stories, and kids were always pissing the bed. I got bullied there a lot – just people being fucking dicks; locking me in the stinking mildewed basement they used to play football in, so I was screaming and shouting, 'Fucking open the door! Open the door!'

I can't be sure exactly how old I was – probably about eight, which is quite early in life to be having a *One Flew Over the Cuckoo's Nest* moment – but there was an incident at Hammerwich which in later life I looked back on as being like a child's version of that film. It was like, 'Matron! *Argh!*'

Trevor was a few years older than me – mixed race like I was, but with darker skin, and only one front tooth. I think they'd stopped him going home one weekend, and he'd jumped up on the snooker table and started singing and dancing in what was at first a light-hearted protest. But the more they tried to get him down, the more he didn't want to know, and then he started swinging this snooker cue around above his head and it all started to get pretty scary. Everyone was shouting and screaming, but I can still pick out whose voice was coming from the record player in the background – it was definitely John Holt singing either 'Help Me Make It Through the Night' or 'Dock of the Bay'.

Either way, it's going to work well if someone ever makes a film of my story. But what was even better was when the situation kind of reached its climax – just before they finally dragged Trevor down off the table and he had to be locked up for a couple of weeks, and when everyone was just thinking, 'Fucking hell!' – there was a pause in the music and the room went silent, then suddenly 'Stay with Me Till Dawn' by Judie Tzuke came on. Someone had decided that this was the right tune to calm the situation down with, and they were right, because I had been scared and then I wasn't.

I've actually been in touch with Judie recently. She's a lovely woman – she was quite taken aback when I told her the string arrangement at the back end of 'Stay with Me Till Dawn' had changed my life for ever. I'm hoping to work with her one day – because that track was definitely one of the starting points for my journey with strings, and I've always thought you could trace a line back from 'Sea of Tears' on *Timeless* to the calming effect her song had on me in that moment of crisis.

The second incident, a few months later, was also quite traumatic. This was after I'd been moved from Hammerwich to Croxdene children's home, when Miss O'Connor said goodbye. I loved Miss O'Connor – she'd been my social worker for years, and she really cared about me. I think they said she'd have to be removed from my case, because there was a possibility – which didn't come to anything – of her adopting me, although it's possible that this memory was just wishful thinking on my part. Either way, while they were doing the paperwork to register my arrival, they put me in this prefab at the bottom of the garden. I think they used to teach lessons in there to the kids that were too naughty to go to school. Anyway, it was quite a lengthy room, maybe 25 foot by 10, with steps that went down at the end to another smaller section, which had a gramophone in it.

I looked through the window, and then I went over to the record player and lifted the lid up. It smelt of electricity, which I hadn't realised till that moment had a smell, and when I looked down at the turntable, the record on the deck was by Supertramp. I pulled the arm across – *ker-klonk* – and released the switch so the needle came over and lowered down onto the vinyl. Then I listened to the record three times, one after the other. It was 'The Logical Song', and I don't know which part got to me – maybe the line where he asks someone to please tell him who he is – but by the end of the third play, I was in bits.

In the short term, there were two basic problems. The first was that I was really unhappy to have come to this new place that I knew I was going to have to adjust to. The second was that I just didn't want Miss O'Connor to go. As a consequence, I was screaming my head off until they came to drag me out of there, and they had to get another one of the people who worked there to come and help do it because one wasn't enough. I watched Miss O'Connor leaving as they took me off to my room, and that was the last time I ever saw her.

What I'd planned to do now was carry on telling you something else and then suddenly switch back and say, 'Didn't you realise? Look at this for sleight-of-hand magic!' But the fact is this fucking time machine which is like a lift shaft up and down between the different floors of my life is too big a part of the story to fuck about with. Because what anyone reading this who is the kind of person who does pub quizzes will already have noticed is that both those tracks – the Supertramp and the Judie Tzuke – actually came out in 1979, which is a good three years after these Hammerwich and Croxdene events took place.

If that's not a time machine doing its job, then I don't know what is. People often misunderstand the nature of metaphor in these kinds of conversations. Like when Sun Ra talked about coming from Saturn, he hadn't got his passport stamped by aliens (at least I don't think he had); that was just a way of preparing you for the fact that he rejected conventional ways of doing things, and wanted to be able to organise information in a pattern that made sense for him. It's the same with me and my time machine. I'm not claiming to be a fucking Timelord, just finding my own way of describing music's power to take you from one place to another.

For example, it makes sense to think of sampling in hip-hop as a kind of time travel – because you capture the moment at which it was originally made and transport it into another context. But I also think the human mind exports music backwards and forwards in time as a kind of lubricant – or an antidote even – for personal trauma. Well, that's what my mind does anyway. Because my inner music supervisor has got together with my inner cinematographer to allocate Judie Tzuke to one distressing scene and 'The Logical Song' to another, and when I go back to those incidents in my mind I experience them through the therapeutic filter of those songs, which I suppose is a way of comforting myself and blunting the impact of the memory, so I hear string arrangements and lyrics rather than feeling fear or desperation or physical pain.

I don't know if everyone does this, or if it's just me. I know my fight or flight mechanism is probably on more of a hair trigger than most people's, and I understand that the trauma in my early life has manifested itself in my drug addiction, but I think the fact that there was no one I could rely on for a reliable timeline of the events in my life has given me a compensatory ability to bring things into sync through sound. Whether that's by using the threads of a song to stitch up the damaged patchwork quilt of my memory, or by directing musicians to make the kind of music I want to hear, it's kind of the same transaction.

The music almost becomes the timeline, and most of the associations I have with it do actually belong in the place and time my mind puts them. Like I know ELO's 'Mr Blue Sky' – another big early strings moment for me – came out in 1977, the year of the Silver Jubilee, because I was at Lew Joseph by then, and I remember having a special Jubilee cup in my hand and waving it when I heard the song. There's also a picture of all the kids at the home gathered round a Union Jack. In fact, here's a poem I wrote about that very patriotic moment. It's called 'My Diary from Hell':

'Stop the fucking noise'
'Stop the fucking noise'
But I won't shut up
I fucking belong here too

Time for dinner
'Wash your hands for dinner'
'Wash your hands for dinner'
'Wash your hands for dinner'

Make sure you say grace –
Let them know how fucking thankful we are
If you behave yourself
You may be able to play your fucking music

So what's it gonna be?
T-Rex or The Stranglers
Why can't I be free
Like 'Jean Genie' and Jean-Jacques Burnel?

Before I change my fucking hairstyle
'Cos The Jam are in their way

But in the meantime
I know every fucking word to *Sergeant Pepper's* . . .

The Hendersons
Will all be there
When I'm 64
1–2–3–4

More dinner
More hands
More knives
More forks
More minutes
More time

Put on your Union Jack hat
It's the Silver Jubilee
Dressed like a cunt
So the whole street can see

Saturday morning pocket money
Ten Number 6 and a packet of chips
Save your change
For a 45 disc

The Stranglers – white vinyl at 33
When I get old will they remember me?
'Just 'cos you feel it doesn't mean it's there'
I heard that somewhere

I feel like I'm gonna fall over today
And really hurt myself

I can really see it
I can almost wish it

Save me from the long grass
Save me from the blades
Save me
From the insane

I can see my home from here
But I don't know how to get there
I can see my home from here
But I don't know how to get there

Ask me where the hell I'm going
One thousand feet per second
Diary of the defunct
Diary of the monk

. . . my diary from hell

The next year, after the Silver Jubilee, we went to Butlin's in Minehead and me and another black kid from the home did a cover of 'Come Back My Love' by Darts – which I always thought was by Showaddywaddy – in shorts and striped t-shirts in the talent contest. Good job that's not on YouTube.

Because I was only eleven in the summer of 1977, I was kind of hanging on the coat-tails of punk, but the one band I really got into were The Stranglers. I bought their first album, *Rattus Norvegicus,* with the money I earned doing odd jobs at the garage round the corner from the home – swabbing up, serving petrol, even a couple of times helping to put stripes on car bodywork. It was like a Saturday job before I got fully into the skating. I can remember the smell of the petrol as I served it at the pump. 'How much, sir?' 'Two pound.' 'OK.' Pour the petrol. Then when the boss Richard went out, me and Andrew, who worked for him and liked punk, would listen to 'Hanging Around' – that was The Stranglers song that really got me, and not just for Christ telling his mother 'not to bother', but also for Jean-Jacques Burnel, baby. His bass sound was blacker and dirtier than the engine oil on our hands.

D2. Dirty and Horrible

So first I came from the Hammerwich children's home to Croxdene, and then from Croxdene I went to Mrs Holden's in Walsall, which was not far away. I didn't realise this at the time – a summer can seem like for ever at that age – but Mrs Holden's was kind of a halfway house, and that year she had another, older black kid named Stephen there who she was looking after too. I was always trying to figure out what my dad would be like based on the picture I had in my head from visits to my mum's house, years before, and seeing that picture of him on her shelf. The guy that was sitting in the chair when I came along was Pusey, who was my mum's lover at the time, and it was like a black man's house: it smelt of smoke, dominoes, a different kind of sweat. So Stephen reminded me of that, in a Proustian kind of way – it was like, 'Ah, black sweat!'

When he'd gone out I used to sniff the collar of his jacket. Come on, kids, gimme a break here, you've all scratched your arse and smelled it a few times in your life. Well, I sniffed collars because I wanted to get in touch with my roots . . . the arse-sniffing would come later. Stephen was always in and out, and I never stopped wanting to know where he was going. One time I saw him coming down the stairs with some skates, and as he went out the door – in the middle of some argument or another – I asked him where he was off to. He just said, 'I'm going roller-drome.'

So that planted a seed.

Stephen was always in trouble, and then he left. The police came one time, and he was gone. I was too young to question why or how anything was happening. All I could see was that Mrs Holden's motivation was good – she was trying to help the kids in her care. Unfortunately, her husband – Mr Holden – was a horrible cunt. He just sat and watched the wrestling. He used to be glued to Mick McManus on a Saturday. He'd be on the edge of his seat, and if you crossed in front of him, when he was smoking his pipe, you'd get a beating. I kind of got used to it.

When I was making the documentary, *When Saturn Returnz*, I went back to the address we'd lived at and knocked on the door, and they said, 'No, don't know who you mean – oh, Mrs Holden, she moved down to another street.' So I went to that house, and whoever lived there said, 'Oh, no, she went to the new maisonettes.' And I went there with the film crew and knocked on the door. In fact, to be more accurate, I pressed every buzzer, saying, 'It's Cliff, it's Cliff.' The buzzer buzzed, the door opened, she said the number – I can't remember which it was – and in I went. She opened the door, and the first thing she said – straight off the bat, and I'm going to try to write this in her Black Country accent, just to give you the flavour of it – was, 'I wondered when yow was cumin'.'

I told her I had a film crew with me and asked if she'd mind if they were there to film us talking. She said, 'No, come on in.' So I sat down with her, and the first thing she said was, 'Oh, I know yow've done really well now. I see yow on the telly.' Then I asked her if it was all right for me to ask her a few questions, and she said, 'Yeah.'

It was good to see Mrs Holden again but as we were talking all these windows and doors flew open in my mind and some very dark memories of that time – which I had battled to hold back throughout my adult life – came flooding in. I felt sick as I remembered the long-term sexual abuse which I suffered during that period of my life at the hands of an older girl.

She was sixteen years old and I was only a little kid – still in Busill Jones junior school, probably only nine but maybe ten at the oldest. The first horrible thing was when this girl pushed me down onto her breast, and then it became worse than that, when I used to have to go down on her. I always remember having fucking pubic hairs in my throat. And it was fucking horrible. Horrible. I didn't know what the fuck was going on, but I knew it wasn't right.

I used to tell her that I knew what was happening was wrong and I was going to tell my social worker, but she used my moral sense against me by telling me it was all my fault and I would get locked up if anyone found out. Once the avenue of telling anyone was closed, my only way of defending myself against my abuser was just to slowly get at her, any way I could. Obviously she had all the power in this situation, but at least by constantly staring at her and whispering in her ear about how what she was doing was wrong, I found a way to fight back, the same way weeds will grow through concrete.

This went on – her abusing me and me trying to get back at her – for about two years, and the consequences in terms of my later relations with women would be fairly horrendous. By the time I finally got away from the Holdens' house, the damage was done. These were my first sexual experiences and they were just too much. Especially with the background of abandonment and me wanting to be mothered. I questioned . . . I didn't even question, I didn't know anything. I just felt dirty and horrible.

D3. Ruby Red's and Whispering Wheels

When my placement with the Holdens ended, the local author-ity moved me away to the Lew Joseph children's home in Wolverhampton, because they couldn't have me staying in the same area. What I needed at that point in my life was some form of escapism, and when I heard soon after I got there that some of the kids from Lew Joseph went to Whispering Wheels on a Tuesday night, that was the little bit of hope I was looking for.

'No way!' I said excitedly. 'That's where Stephen used to go!' Because my endless questioning had finally broken Stephen down to the point where he'd told me that Whispering Wheels was the name of the roller-drome he was always on the way to. The third or fourth time I went I actually saw him there, and called out, 'My brother!' But he just completely ignored me and went straight home, because he was selling weed.

Three or four of us would get a lift over to Whispering Wheels in a tiny Fiat on a Tuesday, and the DJ would be playing music. His name was Jacko and he turned out to be mates with the guy who ran the local record shop, Ruby Red's. Previous to that I would have just gone to the local Boots store to buy singles from the rack – interim shit. Suddenly I was hearing Jacko playing all this new music that I'd not discovered before – 'September' by Earth, Wind and Fire; KC and the Sunshine Band; even Boney M's 'Brown Girl in the Ring' – I guess now you'd think of it as pop r'n'b, but at the time it was pretty much disco. This made a big impression on me because it was different to the new wave and punk I'd been hearing in the predominantly white environ-ments that I'd been living in, and I wanted to know where it came from, so I walked up the steps to where Jacko was playing records – I've never thought of it this way before, but I suppose this was my first experience of seeing what a DJ did – and asked him, 'Where'd you get that from?' 'Well, I got that from Ruby Red's.'

So Whispering Wheels guided me to Ruby Red's, and that was how I started to discover soul music. Because Jacko would be playing Odyssey, The Gap Band's 'Oops Upside Your Head' at the roller-drome – because if whichever auntie and uncle were on duty at Lew Joseph's weren't being cunts, they'd let me go there at the weekend too, when most of the other kids got to go home but I didn't.

We'd skate round to Ruby Red's, which was on the outside of the Mander shopping centre, and Jacko turned out to be a mate of Mick the owner, so we were allowed in there on our skates and he'd show us what the records he'd played were, and we'd go through all the 12-inch singles. It was an important transition for me to go from buying 7-inch picture sleeves by The Jam and Squeeze to maybe a 12-inch single by Shalamar, or 'Behind the Groove' by Teena Marie.

Getting those records was a big thing for me, but the skating was a big thing too . . . I was really fucking good at skating, man; I still am. Quads only, please – four wheels – thank you. Once I started going to Whispering Wheels regularly, I got friendly with a guy everyone called 'Cockney' – because he came from London – who was a great skater. He was the baddest – the best at Whispering Wheels, always had the girl. There was another unbelievable little skater called Kenny. He thought he was the best too, but he wasn't. Cockney took care of that. Anyway, we'd hang around there together on the Saturday, play the lone Space Invader machine, get hot snacks. That was how the roller-hockey started, but that's another story.

The point is that when it comes to your musical heritage, you are what you eat, and what I was eating had started to change. I'd take my singles home from Ruby Red's to Lew Joseph, and play them on a Sunday. You'd keep your stuff in these kind of rustic brown lockers. There were forty-two of them, and the records you'd put in were what defined who you were. Now this mad new world was opening up for me. Even though you weren't meant to, we'd skate in the Mander Centre. The flooring was amazing – it was smooth as eggs. Me, Cockney and Mitchell – the son of Whispering Wheels' owner – would skate round there all day and security would chase us. We'd go down the spiral to the second floor, it was the bollocks. In the end they had to put up shutters to stop us going in.

D4. Gofer the Goalie Finds His Way Home

I'd noticed them putting these nets up when I was hanging around at Whispering Wheels after skating on a Saturday, and then one of the guys said, 'Do you want to stick around and watch the hockey?' It turned out Jacko the DJ played roller-hockey, as did Cockney and Kenny and Mitchell. It didn't take long before I was playing too.

Because I was one of the younger kids there and trying hard to be in with everyone, they used to call me 'Gofer' – 'Go for this, go for that.' So when the cry went up, 'Who's going to go in goal?' it was inevitably going to end up being me. No one in their right mind would take that job out of choice – and I also had the bad memories of going to Busill Jones junior school for the first time after being in Hammerwich. It was afternoon by the time I got there, they were doing sport, and I got thrown straight in goal. The first shot that came in someone nutmegged me and I was the fucking embarrassment of the school. I'd failed once again.

Luckily, it turned out that as a roller-hockey goalkeeper I was the fucking bollocks. We went all round the country in the league. We used to go to Loughborough; Leicester had a great team then, too, but we were doing some fucking damage. Believe it or not, we were so good we got called up for the England roller-hockey B-team. Then we went to Rhyl, or somewhere on the Welsh coast, to play in a competition. This was me, Kenny and Cockney, and we ended up being pulverised by Farnham. They were licking shots, man, and it was a different kind of shot. We were getting punished. But I was a good keeper, and this was

a new thing for me – to be travelling around the country being good at something. I guess it laid the foundation stone for being in a breakdancing crew (which I wasn't that good at) and graffiti (which I was) a bit later on.

Roller-hockey was a hard sport. You could smell the sweat in the changing rooms even before the game started. You fucking went out there and you worked hard, or you got pummelled. Or sometimes you worked hard and you got pummelled anyway. I was always balanced on my heels and my toe-stops. I think that's why the posture in yoga that we call 'Awkward' – for obvious reasons, because you're almost seated, but on your toes – comes easily to me: because I spent so much time in that position playing roller-hockey.

I was always in goal, never an outfield player, but I'd get a stick and play around with Kenny. He was good – he'd move you one way and then the other – but I was quick too. You couldn't catch me. I started working at Whispering Wheels on a Saturday, to get my membership, because you had to pay a fee for the roller-hockey. I was serving skates – 'Give me your shoes,

At Busill Jones junior school. My best friend Paul Gough is standing right in front of me

The Supreme Graffiti Team meeting Henry Chalfant for the first time at Heath Town precinct

The only school picture of me in my glasses

In the Chelsea Hotel, on the Lower East Side – a different kind of educational establishment

Me, Birdie, Brim Fuentes and Bio (or Wilfredo Valenciano, to give him his real name) outside Nicholls Paints, PPG Automotive, in Walsall

Spinning on my head with the Wolverhampton B-Boys breakdance crew. Don't ask me to do this now, although I will still give it a go

Outside Seen's aerosol shop

Straight outta the Kangol catalogue on the mean streets of Willenhall

On the subway at Grand Concourse, 149th Street, New York

With Vulcan, T-Kid, Bio, Nicer, Brim and 3D. We'd painted a fake subway train at Sun Street studio as prep for the Birmingham Library graffiti exhibition

Ultimate B-boy pose in three-quarter ice-wash goose down, Fordham Road, the Bronx

With my mum and my brothers Stuart and Jo Jo, in my mum's back yard at 26 North Street, Walsall

In the Queen's back yard at Buckingham Palace

Doing yoga in Ibiza

I had a dream too. 'Don't wish too hard, kid, 'cos it might come true'

With Doc Scott and GQ at the Metalheadz boat party at the 2014 Outlook Festival. The dark lord Sith lurks – as always – in the background

Clockwise from top left: Mika at Stonehenge; Chance – she's leaving home; Koko stows away; the treehouse in Thailand; why the long face?

I'll go and get your size.' I'd often be there on a Sunday too, till I was kind of part of the furniture. I lived on skates for a couple of years. Wouldn't take them off. I'd skate on the bus, skate home, whatever.

Once I started going to Whispering Wheels on a Sunday night, there'd be way more black people there. The music was more of a reggae sound, the place smelled of weed, and there was a lot of hustling going on. Guys would pull up outside in three-litre Ford Capris. A guy called Stepford was kind of running things – a black guy with a big afro – he was the deputy manager and he was seeing Mitchell's sister, so that was kind of his in. There'd always be big bass noise when he was around.

Things were getting heavier on the rink as well. On Sundays we'd do a thing called 'Figure of eight', which basically meant taking people out. Me, Cockney and Kenny were a bit of a tag-team and people were getting smacked – until it started getting really nasty and someone got a broken leg. Big people wanted to fight me, but no one dared take Cockney on because that guy was not a joke.

After skating we started going to the Half Moon Club, which was where all the black guys from the estate would hang out listening to reggae. That was amazing, but I never realised at the time how many of them were into brown – they were heroin addicts, but you didn't see this so you didn't know. The Half Moon was round the corner from where my mum lived. She'd come to the home and I'd visited her a couple of times – I'd look down from her balcony and see the same Ford Capris from Whispering Wheels pull up in front of the blocks on the estate.

Back at the children's home, I could look out of the window from the TV room and see the shopping arcade – the Mander Centre. One day I just thought, 'Fuck it, I'm going to run,' so I did. I ran away to my mum's, and when I turned up there she just said, 'I knew you were going to come one day.' I think I was approaching eighteen by that time, but it was still kind of like I was on the run. One time at the rink someone told me, 'The police are here and they're coming for you.' The rink was dark but I was scouting round to catch a glimpse of them. Next thing I knew all these guys in jackets were just chasing me while I was on my fucking skates. Bam, I'm on the floor, and they carted me off back to the home in the police car. But the next time I ran away back to Mum's I'd turned eighteen and there was nothing they could do. Haile Selassie was about to get a new recruit.

D5. 'Faffinations'

We decided between ourselves, me and my wife Mika, that when it came to bringing up our daughter Koko – who is five years old at the time of writing – we would rather have her believe in fucking unicorns than something she thinks she has to go along with because she's in fear of it. I want her to be spiritual in a way that encourages her to be kind to other people, because to me that is what real religion should be – a structure within which you and your loved ones can embrace spirituality. That's why we love the Buddhism that surrounds us in Thailand so much: because it doesn't have the same kind of rules so many other religions have.

So if you ask me about religion, no thank you; but when you talk to me about spirituality, I'm all ears. It would be different if all religions were tolerant of each other and respected the spiritual buffer zone where one faith moves into another. There are places in the world where that happens, and Thailand is one of them, because the Muslim community there is – by and large – tolerant of Buddhism; even though the two religions are completely different, they manage to co-exist in the same place, harmoniously.

At the bottom of the hill where I live, there's this really beautiful place where all these cats – actual cats, not humans in jive talk – live. One of them looks like Genghis Khan – he's got this little white moustache that goes all the way down the side of his face, and he's funny as fuck. So there's Genghis and his cat courtiers sitting around – in a yard full of cockerels and chickens, just there, shooting the breeze. Now I'm not saying there's nowhere in England – probably a farmyard somewhere – where the cats and the chickens get on together but, as a general rule, if I put a chicken in the fucking 'hood, in an urban community with a few more chickens, then I put a few cats in there, the chickens are going to get ripped to shreds. Let's say I put a pit-bull that's been trained to be vicious and vindictive in that same fucking room, and I throw a fucking sausage dog and a little Chihuahua and a baby in there, well, something's going to go wrong, isn't it? Maybe if I put them all in together from the very start of their journey, they could manage to be harmonious. I don't know. Try it with your own Chihuahua, but maybe hold off on the baby.

When I was in foster-care as a kid with Mr and Mrs Jones, they used to force me to go to Sunday school. The same people that forced me to go to Sunday school were letting their son put a fucking dog's lead around my neck and walk me around the front room with it . . . and it wasn't long after that I got placed with the Holdens and ended up being abused. So for me, as a kid, that was confusing. 'Hey, I've got to get my cock out as a fucking young boy and be molested or get pulled around the front room in a dog collar, but then you go to church on Sunday and that makes it all right, does it?' Really? What kind of fucking religion's that? Ah, don't start me off.

I guess it's the same kind of religion that allows someone in the Mafia to think, 'Let's just go and murder everyone Monday to Friday because it's our job to go and collect money and do shit and put the vice on motherfuckers, but on Sunday we'll just go and do twenty Hail Marys and we'll be forgiven for it.' The deathbed confession is another good one – 'Hey, listen, Fred West. You're a wicked serial killer but if you want to turn Catholic on your deathbed after you've murdered everyone, all will probably be forgiven and you'll probably go to heaven.'

Do you really think that fucking God sits there and goes, 'You, Clifford Joseph Price' – let's use another name because I might be a special case – 'You, Jonathan Dimbleby from Scunthorpe . . . you've been a good man all your life but I notice you don't have a wedding band on, so you will burn in hell, because you should be married. Look at my wedding ring. Yes, I, God, wear a wedding ring also.' Can you fucking get your head around this shit? Come on, guys: it's a fucking bubble. You're having a bubble.

Of course some people might be slightly offended by what I say. And, to be quite frank, I don't give a fuck. I'm just giving you my opinion about religion, which is that I think it's the biggest killer on the planet.

You could say it's AIDS or Ebola or SARS, or you could say it's the bubonic plague, but I say stop trying to stigmatise the Black Death. Religion's a fucking killer disease, because it eradicates self-knowledge and makes you conform to something whether or not you think it's true. Truth is about being true to yourself and treating other people well, whereas this is like these magic shows from Vegas where you watch them and think, 'Wow, it's like Imagination said, it's just a fucking illusion.' Yeah, there's a certain amount of shit in it that could be quite fun and loveable, but the hard fact is that forcing particular religions on people for whom it's not part of their culture has created a lot of fucking war over the centuries, man. That's why I say religion is the biggest killer.

Isn't it weird how many of the most traumatised and violent places on earth tend to be the ones where really fanatical religions are calling the shots? But then when you try to find out why these fanatics believe in something so much, the reason will usually tend to be some crazy shit like, 'Tell you what, I'm going to be so fucking fanatical because I want twenty virgins when I die.'

It just makes no sense, because whatever idea you have of a spirit world when you die, it's obvious that we don't take this body with us. Or is your body going to magically reappear and all of a sudden you're going to have a really great cock because you died in the course of committing an act of terrorism? Do me a fucking favour.

I think that a lot of people who are fanatics within particular religions – or political movements for that matter – are in denial anyway, and pretty much fucking hate themselves deep down because they don't know the answers, and they're never going to either. What they need to do is to let it go. Because none of us has those answers. None of us can really definitively say, 'This is how the universe came about,' much as we might like to know.

To me, the ironies of religion and humankind are like watching TV in another country, in another language. You know it makes sense to the people who live there, but that doesn't stop it looking ridiculous. As I'm saying that, I can imagine aliens sitting on another planet going, 'Fuck, those humans we farmed twenty million light years away are fucking stupid, aren't they? We were right to throw in that bit of religious belief to keep them confused and fighting among themselves. Let's just keep raping all the gold out of the planet, and when it's completely exhausted, we won't even have to blow it up, because they'll probably do that themselves.' Now this might sound like complete bollocks to you, but to me it makes no less sense than a lot of the things millions of people believe.

What life is all about, whether you have religious affiliations or not, is trying to balance those thoughts. When I'm trying to do that, I often remind myself of the story about the Buddhist monk inside someone's house who picks up the object, the shiny object that doesn't belong to him, and places it in his pocket, and his left hand grabs his right hand and makes his right hand take it back out of his pocket and put it back: *it's not yours*.

I think it's very important, that process of defusing, detaching, disengaging . . . what's the word when a spaceship loses a piece? 'Jettison'? I love that word, 'jettison'. I want to jettison all of these old ways of mine, these patterns, to try to become a better person. But I don't believe that religion holds any of keys to that process. I almost think we have to pick the locks of those doors ourselves to find our way through and out of the tower of fucking Babel that religion has created for us. Because a lot of these filters of incoherence and incomprehension that shroud us from our true selves were actually put there by the people who claim to be helping us.

Surely Jesus – this guy that, you know, probably existed but they kind of made it up and layered it on a little bit – might have had a bit of a *tan*, because he lived where he lived? Slightly? Or maybe he didn't like the sun. You know? It's all of these things that I think about – Jesus being black, like Beethoven (which is another story), the rewriting of the King James version of the Bible, which was not unlike the way great films will be barbarised by Hollywood remakes that give you complete faffinations of the originals.

Obviously that's a word I've made up, from when my mum used to say, 'Oh, stop faffing around.' I've always thought the people who come up with these religious stories to reflect their own view of the world and then try to present them as universal, they're faffinating. So all of these Hollywood movie-style faffinations – the impossible demigodness of them, if that's even the right word – sometimes that takes away from the actual storyline. And the actual storyline as far as I'm concerned is to take a moment and ask yourself, 'How can me version 2.1 be better than me version 2.0 was yesterday? How can I grow? How can I get there in the end?' And then suddenly you realise that there is no end – that's all part of the Beautiful Accident.

ALL THINGS REMEMBERED

Since *Timeless* was very much a coming-of-age album for me
– and a very rose-tinted record for a lot of people who loved it
when it came out – *The Journey Man*, by definition, had to sur-
pass it. Because whatever else I am or am not now, I'm definitely
of age. It was also important because of the way music has gone,
with DJs being the new rock stars and getting paid and claiming
the fame for pushing buttons . . . I'm not saying that's wrong for
the people that deserve it. I've never been a great DJ myself, but
the great DJs were and are my peers – Randall, Grooverider,
Fabio, Doc Scott . . . Marcus Intalex was a great DJ too. But
since I'm not one of them I had to find a way of leapfrogging all
of that. And the best way for me to do so with *The Journey Man*
was to try to create an album that was also my life story – sixteen
tracks long, sixteen shades of my life, somehow finding a way
to decipher what the twelve people round the table in my head
(eleven adults, but one of them still just a boy) would agree to,
and not agree to, at times . . .

It goes without saying that I just wanted to push the envelope.
I wanted to put the Ferrari fucking sideways. I really needed to
push that car, man – push that fucking engine. And in trying to
do that I was obviously inspired by the greats. I looked at 3D
from Massive Attack. Robert Del Naja, to give him his full name
– or 'Delje' (which is what everyone calls him) – has been a good
friend of mine for years, since we were in *Bombin'* together in the
eighties. And there's no denying what Massive Attack achieved
in terms of coming out of The Wild Bunch with the ethos of the
samples, and pushing the boundaries of the sample and the loop

in terms of almost the world-music aspect of it. Whether you want to call that 'trip-hop', or whatever, when *Blue Lines* came out in 1991 it was definitely an amazing way of encompassing the previous ten years of sound. So I kind of used that as my first benchmark, thinking, 'OK, this is something to aspire to.'

But I also looked at my own *Timeless*. Now *Timeless* is a very beautiful blueprint, but in terms of the morality of it – and I don't mean the mortality, I mean the morality – *Timeless* was this beautiful redskin girl in the ghetto. Not a Native American; 'redskin' is a Jamaican word for the girl you'd always be looking at – fit as you like, fit as fuck, man, like . . . I would approach her, but she's pushing a pram, and that means she's got a man. That means someone else is courting her. It means if I want to go anywhere near her, I've got to know what I'm doing, because the kid's three years old: 'Woah, hang on a minute, this is a seasoned honey right here, and I've got to be really careful how I approach that.' Because it's in the 'hood, as well; you know she's fit, so you know she's got to have some ranks.

Timeless was always like that – she's pushing this pram and always smiling and being very beautiful and emitting great energy – but to me it had begun to seem like that beautiful girl became an addict. She got weary and there were black lines around her eyes – the panda eyes, like Joy Regan had – and she'd turned into an alcoholic, until she just sat down on the fucking kerbside looking worn out and beat up. She didn't care how she looked any more. And all of a sudden the pram she's pushing was a wheelchair, and in the fucking wheelchair was this fucking drooling kid with locked-in syndrome, because that's what the scene had become for me.

In the last ten years this music that I love with a fucking passion had become gentrified within the machine of the music industry. So *The Journey Man* for me had to be like this big

　　　　　　　　ALL THINGS REMEMBERED

brother that came along and just comforted the redskin sister – picked her up, saying, 'Look, it's going to be all right. You go home, have a long fucking bath. It will freshen you up, and you'll still look beautiful.'

But as for the kid, the big brother wants to pick the fucking kid up out of that fucking wheelchair and just slap him round the face and say, 'Yo! I know you can fucking walk, because I've seen you fucking walk. You didn't get hit by a car, you didn't get hit by a meteorite, you're just faking it, sitting in a fucking chair, drooling, getting sweets put in front of you because everyone feels sorry for you. I know you can fucking walk. So what I want you to do is go home, don't look over your fucking shoulder, and start making the fucking music that's really in your heart. And get rid of that ridiculous Hoxton sideways Hitler haircut while you're at it.'

Maybe people might think I'm being too hard on myself there. Or maybe that this is the wrong metaphor to use 'because the kid in the wheelchair's happy'. Now if the kid had a good reason for being in that wheelchair because he was paralysed or disabled or something – well, that would obviously be a totally different thing. But I saw this kid running for a bus the other day! I know he doesn't need to be in there. Maybe a more politically correct way of putting it might be if a friend of yours had a kid that you knew was totally sound in mind and body, but his mum was still pushing him around in a pushchair at six years old. Or pulling him round on reins! That's how drum 'n' bass has gone, and it shouldn't have to be like that.

And I know that as well as anyone, because I was that redskin girl, and I was that kid in the pram. I was so out of it and such a fucking addict that I actually managed to become a metaphor for myself. That's what me cleaning up and going to Thailand was about – becoming my own big brother so my inner spirit could save me from the bullshit that this music's become. Why should drum 'n' bass music be looked at like some fucking remedial? Why should it be this thing that you almost feel embarrassed by if you were to sit an artist from another country in a chair and play him your fucking music – having to make excuses about the way that it sounds? I didn't want to have that feeling any more, because I believe the music that I make that comes from this genre is mature enough to stand on its own two feet and go fifteen fucking rounds with any other kind of music you care to put in the ring with it.

Why should it be marginalised and become the subject of plagiarism by the very people it spawned? Because when you hear my band onstage at Ronnie Scott's you can forget about drum 'n' bass. You start to think, 'It sounds like Latin dance music,' or, 'It sounds like punk,' or, 'It sounds like a full-on fucking rock band, really going at it.' And that's how it should be. Because that's the destination *The Journey Man* was heading for all along – to blow the frame out of the computer, take away that fucking square, and remind yourself that it's not a closed cardboard box, it's an infinite space within which you can move around and do anything you fucking want.

SIDE E

E1. An 18-Rated *Truman Show*

Even setting aside the Beautiful Accident, which I've gone into elsewhere, three of the biggest creative gear-changes in my life have come about through appearing on TV programmes. Being in *Bombin'* kick-started my whole career, and learning to conduct an orchestra and putting together *Goldie's Band* – where I first came across the great Natalie Duncan – were a couple more really important artistic way-posts on the journey for me. Those last two deserve chapters of their own, but I also want to say a bit about a few of the less critically respectable shows I've been on.

I've never felt I had anything to apologise for in terms of deciding to appear on *Celebrity Big Brother* or *Strictly Come Dancing* or *Come Dine with Me* or *All Star Mr & Mrs* or any of the lesser ones. In terms of people going, 'Why were you on that?' I just simply don't give a fuck. Because of being in care, my life's been documented since the age of three, so privacy's never really been an issue for me. Having ten social workers deciding your destiny like it's some kind of 18-rated *Truman Show* will do that to a person. My life's been a reality TV show, so do you think being observed by a couple of other human beings that are lesser gods than me can really affect my fucking sense of self at this stage?

No one can accuse me of doing them for ego reasons either, because I'm always the first one to be voted out. *Celebrity Big Brother 2* – first out. *Strictly* – first out, even though I was a not world-beating but still competition-standard breakdancer. I mean, apart from the money – which always comes in handy – I almost think I do them because I want to take the piss. When you've grown up in a children's home with forty-two kids, all of whom are searching for the truth, and then suddenly you're in a house on TV with ten adults who are all pretending they don't know who they are, it just kind of makes you want to be the cat among the pigeons.

Some people have said to me that some of my early exits – and especially not winning the conducting show – were down to racism on the part of the voting public, but I prefer to think of the reason as being that real people make the audience (and the programme makers) uncomfortable. *Strictly* was kind of a special case, because there was some press thing where somebody was being biased about something, and I refused to do it, and this producer said, 'Right, OK,' and I said, 'You know what? Fuck you!' She said, 'What did you say?' I repeated, 'Fuck you.' And that was it. I strongly suspected I'd be gone at the first possible opportunity. It's just what happens, isn't it? You know how game shows work. I don't mind that.

The great thing is, if you're first off, you still get paid. Put the monkey on the barrel and turn the handle, but the smart monkey fucks off sharpish with the cash, and that way you know the music and the art will never get compromised.

E2. Onstage at Ronnie Scott's

Ah, man! Where am I? Wow. I'm onstage, at Ronnie Scott's, surrounded by an unbelievable band, and the alchemy's so powerful that I can influence the drummers with my own hands. I
can look at Matt Calvert and vibe and jam and see they're all
on the same wavelength. I can look at the keyboard player, Sam
Crowe, and he just gets it. And I can look over at Dan Nicholls
and Dan's vibing on the SH101 bassline and he's improvising
as I'm throwing the energy at him. And then I can just bury my
head in the kick drum and go at it full leather, full iron with
Adam Betts – the first of two maniac fucking drummers who
have really changed my life. And then I can look at John Blease
– the other one of those two drummers – and Blease is banging
his brushes, and I can just roll my fingers, straight eye contact,
we just connect, and we can really zoom into the detail of the
alchemy.

Then the various singers come into it, and none of them are
taking any prisoners either. Terri Walker's one of them. She
phoned me up a while before the gig and said, 'I didn't get it
before, but I get it now. I knew I was singing the song, I knew
I was singing the words, but the meaning of it didn't really resonate with me, like the vibration that it gave has just really
kicked in.' And there she is onstage at Ronnie Scott's, totally
taking ownership of the song.

At other times, I can extend my hand out to Natalie Duncan
– who is the muse of my musical universe – I can hold my hand
out at the beginning of 'Redemption' and I can just guide her
exactly where I want the note placed, and extend it to the sky.

You see, where I am is where it's at for me. It's the place I knew I wanted to be twenty-three years ago — at the heart of this alchemy, which is so detailed.

Closing your eyes and realising music is about opening them and living the dream, because this is real electronic music, played live, completely live: the Séancic Method brought to life — in real time. Not midi-track, click-track, backing drums laid over with a drummer who looks like he's really good, or somebody sitting behind a fucking black box, pushing buttons that do very little and claiming the grace and the mannerisms and all of the accolades as if they were their own when they're not.

When it came to playing live there was always this question of: 'What does Goldie do? What does he do onstage? He doesn't play an instrument, so what does he do? Does he simply go behind a black box and look smart, with an orchestra behind him, nodding his head, pretending, or, you know, winning an Oscar?' No. Pushing buttons was never for me. Yeah, I push buttons when I'm DJing, that's what monkeys do, but I'm a gorilla, and not just any gorilla — I'm one gorilla that wants to get the bus out of fucking town and go and live in the fucking jungle.

Because it's about taking this to the extreme, which isn't really extreme, it's where we should have always been. I think electronic music — this sleight-of-hand magic — also lies to itself a little bit. It's very easy to take things so far and then stop — 'It's made on computers, so it should stay on computers, having a laptop open in the middle of a fucking orchestra's cool.' Nah, it's not, you know?

Once you've decided not to settle for that, the easy option is to just transcribe things very directly — 'Let's lay this out and go through the numbers.' But for me that seems a little bit like driving a Ferrari at forty fucking kilometres an hour. It wasn't fucking made for that. I think sometimes people have been in the sun for too long, as well. They kind of lose their way with what it's all about; they get bleached out. I like being a bit more underground, a bit darker in the shadows. I like the sun sometimes, but only to walk through, not to sit in – the dead of night is when things really get done.

I said to Pete Tong way back in the early nineties that I saw this music with orchestras. They all laughed at me, but they're all doing it now. I'm glad it wasn't the fourteenth century, because they'd have probably fucking drowned me for being a witch – 'I see the future, with orchestras and people playing electronic music with an orchestra!' 'Burn him!' That's kind of what it feels like. But if you burnt me then you should basically burn Detroit down, because all of those niggers had some great insight. All of my boys – Mad Mike, Underground Resistance – we knew what was coming, we knew that this was the future. The godfathers of Detroit techno, making that big leap to Europe, being bastardised for whatever reason and gentrified, it was always inevitable. That's why Mad Mike has had to move his studio three times.

I did the live tours with Perry Farrell and Jane's Addiction, also in the nineties, but that was just Yamaha 01s with the backing beats, and certain breaks you'd play over the top. We had a Bose speaker with a click-track coming out of it, and everyone's cued up. I guess that's kind of the precursor to the stage a lot of people are at now, where they've got Ableton performance software to basically run the show for them – they've got it all Abletoned up and whatever else. I just felt, like, 'Take the fucking stabilisers off, man.' To me the music is so epic that it deserves something bigger and better.

I went to the Roundhouse once and saw someone playing drum 'n' bass with a band, and it's basically just a fucking set of drums, but the drummer's drumming to a backing track of drums. I just don't get the fucking point. Just put the fucking drumsticks down and stop fucking miming. Who are you, Marcel Marceau? I guess from their point of view, better the circus you know than the one you don't, right? But for me it's like watching your kid pedalling fast on a bike with stabilisers on: it just doesn't look right. Or your kid going round a corner, leaning the wrong way – going round a right-hand corner, leaning to the left, and still making it. It's not supposed to be possible.

My opinion is that if you're going to do that – these days – you might as well just be sitting there with a laptop, because it becomes a façade. I don't really like the idea of that. I like the idea that if you're going to fucking play live, you should play completely live, everything triggered by humans and that's it. Bar zero, ready, four, three, two, one – if no one starts playing a fucking instrument, there's silence for the entire show. Because no one's in a position to trigger anything where they just press 'start' and it carries on till it ends.

Each to their own, I guess. If people like it, and they get away with it, yeah, it's OK. But it kind of sticks you to a fucking Velcro board; it doesn't really give you any freedom. It certainly doesn't give you the jazz and the music. I saw some techno being done with an orchestra in Paris, and it was good, but it just didn't do it for me. There's a very simple way of doing it where it stays very linear, and of course strings sound great by default – they always do. Even Gary Glitter's 'My Gang' would sound good with strings on, but I'm not sure I want to be in that gang any more.

So if you look at something like my track 'Sea of Tears', then you can just play the string section. But what's the rest of the orchestra doing? What are the flutes doing? What is the brass doing? What are the tubas doing? Is there anything that's being done in that situation where you think it's really utilising what orchestration is?

The time this whole thing really picked up momentum for

me was while I was doing *Timeless* that way at the South Bank a few years ago. The turning point was a very important phone call from Chris Wheeler, the Heritage Orchestra's producer, telling me there was an opportunity to work with them. God bless James Lavelle and Jane Beese for asking me to do that, and Matt Calvert for helping me take the music apart and put it back together. Him and Chris Wheeler's Heritage Orchestra are just on another fucking level, man, for me. And what's happening onstage at Ronnie Scott's is like the concentrate of that Royal Festival Hall show – the intense syrup you'd make squash out of. Of course, standing up inside a band and playing is a great thing in itself, but seeing music that's been translated from an idea spawned within electronica and has now been notated and spread around so that these other human beings can do their own thing with it, which is also my thing . . . I find this manifestation remarkable. That's my kind of alchemy.

I always wanted to play an instrument, but I think because the bad experiences of my childhood had kind of inverted me in terms of how I related to the world, what I did as a kid was make a model of a guitar rather than actually play one. Because I wanted to do art and create things, I made a model guitar out of brass welding-rod stems and plyboard, and I used to mime along to The Stranglers' *Rattus Norvegicus* on it. Even then I was taking the idea of musicianship very seriously without actually being a musician myself. As I got older I always felt my love of music was best expressed by *not* playing an instrument.

What used to get me once I started to make music of my own was knowing that musicians spend twenty years learning a guitar, or thirty years learning how to play a fucking Hammond or a trumpet – they work so hard for the craft of jazz, the craft of their music. So seeing how lazy people would get with it electronically just seemed like a slap in the face to them. I think if the jazz world acted the same as the electronic world, we'd have 256 Kenny Gs and one Miles Davis in the corner, cursing. Because when you think of all the great players in jazz – going back from Kamasi Washington now to Miles Davis and Sonny Rollins and Charles Mingus and Stan Getz and all of them – you're looking at all these people who are giant oaks with great branches in a really big forest. But now in electronic music and dance music we've got all these little saplings that are planted much too close to each other. Everyone's thinking, 'Yeah, we'll plant a few seeds and the trees will grow.' But the wood's weak, you know?

I always thought that with all the possibilities there are within electronica, we should be pushing the envelope a little more, and integrating those human players back into that. Why does the best music from the seventies and eighties still sound so good, even though some of the technology it was made with was really basic? Because there's room for more of the soul to come through, that's why. So now actually being able to bring some of that soul back onstage is the most special thing I've ever been involved in – it's just so fucking powerful.

E3. Chalk Drawings of My Horribly Swollen Penis

When I was at Busill Jones junior school, between the ages of maybe eight and eleven – first while I was at Croxdene and then Mrs Holden's – my best mate was a kid called Paul Gough. We're still in touch forty years later, even though we lost contact at first when I was moved to Lew Joseph. Paul lives in Germany now and plays in some kind of fucking tribute band – I don't know who it's a tribute to, AC/DC or someone quite mad. Anyway, it was always a foregone conclusion that Goughy was going to end up in Deutschland, because he was obsessed with the helmets and uniforms from World War II as a kid. All he would draw in art class were pictures of Stukas. German mad, he was.

We used to go to a shop in an arcade on North Street, Walsall, and even though I wasn't allowed to live with my mum then, I knew she lived nearby – though it might as well have been a million miles away for all the good that knowledge was doing me. We'd buy Airfix models and toy cowboys and Indians – the former for Paul, the latter for me, obviously. We'd go back to Paul's house to assemble the kits, then go up the road to build a camp on the bridge and play with them there. This was just past the garage where I ended up getting the Saturday job with Richard and Andrew.

Paul's mother was seeing an Indian guy then, which at that time was considered to be a bit wrong – you're white, you're not supposed to do that. Her lipstick was a bit mental as well. She looked like Myra Hindley. The first time we met was at the bottom of his garden – which was out the back of Croxdene – when I climbed over the fence and ran into his house. Paul told his mum, 'He's run away,' and she said, 'You've got to get him back, you've got to get him back,' and then she took me back to the home in her car.

I was meant to be the troubled one, but Goughy was like a junior Hermann Göring – he was a sadistic little fuck. One of his favourite things to do was wait till his mum's butter dish was empty, then wash it out and bury it in the rockery till a load of black beetles had gathered in there. Then he'd get a load of ants and throw them in, just to watch them battle! In any war game he'd always have to be the Nazi, while I was already buying into the Native American side of things. Funny how that shit starts early. Our games of Nazis and Indians were like a mid-seventies version of *Alien vs Predator*.

One time the people in charge at Croxdene let me have a sleepover at Goughy's house, camping in the garden. When we were out there we found this bird flapping around with a broken wing – it was speckled, so I think it was a starling. Instead of torturing this bird like you're probably expecting, we were both really excited about trying to save it – 'Fuck, this is our chance; we've got to look after it.' So we got it some water and tried to feed it, made it a bed out of tissues in this shoebox Paul had and put it out in the back garden. I remember going to check on it in the morning, the feel of the dew in the air after you've slept out all night. I opened the box and the starling just fucking died of shock, right there and then. Dead as a doornail. I don't always look my best in the mornings, but this was the worst review I've ever had.

There was another time when me and Goughy were jumping around, just having a laugh, and I climbed up on his shoulders. Unfortunately he fucking fell and I knocked myself out on his grate. That was the first time I'd ever seen stars, at least until years later, when I got a good kicking while I was out with the

Wolverhampton football mob – the Subway Army. The Hardings – Terry and Paddy – they lived up to their name all right. Terry was naughty. I was running with the Sketchley Crew – they knew the meaning of steaming – until one day the boot was on the other foot, but that's another story. If you like all that gangster shit, there's a lot more of it in my first book, *Nine Lives*.

Those days were still a long way off that time I was spark out in Goughy's fireplace. Now when I look back on those happy days with Paul, they kind of feel like my actual childhood – the experience of just being a kid – which got pushed to one side too soon because of the sexual abuse. Across the road from Goughy's house there was a pork scratchings factory, and me, Goughy and a kid called David Poole (who supplied the rope for our great escapes) used to go in and buy them for five pence a bag. Those pork scratchings were my fucking madeleines. We'd eat the scratchings and then we'd climb the fence and, before we knew it, we'd gone too far and were into the yard and then inside the factory next door. I remember there was a tub full of coils of metal – little bits of stuff that you weren't really sure what they were for, they were just parts of the machines. That was what the West Midlands was all about in those days. People made shit. Next thing I knew I was on the lathe and the whole room was full of the smell of Swarfega. It's not exactly fucking *Harry Potter*, is it? But as far as childhoods go, it was a start.

Unfortunately, it was around this time that the abuse began, and that suddenly got me realising that I had a penis. This probably happened a few years before it should've done, because I was constantly masturbating even though my balls hadn't dropped yet, so I couldn't actually come. That was a horrible feeling, and it reached a point where I was actually doing myself damage.

One day I woke up in the Holdens' house and my bell-end had swollen up like the spaceship in *Space 1999*. The shaft was like the empty cargo vessel docking and what you had on top was pure sci-fi. When Goughy came round, I said, 'I'm sorry, I've got to show you something,' and gave him a quick look at it for the purposes of science. Next morning I undid the latch of the gate onto the street and saw that the pavement was covered in chalk drawings of my horribly swollen penis. Yeah, thanks for that, Paul. Remind me to get you back one day . . .

E4. Here Be Baby Dragons

I've been using cocaine – on and off, but mostly on – for thirty-five years. If I was to carry on at the rate I was going before, my heart would fucking explode. Because when I talk about drug use, I mean hardcore drug use – you know, half an ounce. So having struggled with addiction through pretty much my whole adult life, I would say the three-and-a-half-month period of not using I had around the latter stages of making *The Journey Man* was one of the longest clean periods I've had in my entire earthly existence.

In terms of that one-on-one fight with the dragon where you sometimes think you're getting on top of him but he always comes back, this is the first time I've dared to feel like I might have actually won. Well, to be honest, I have felt like that before, but something would always shore him up and he'd come back stronger just when I thought I'd finished him off. This time, instead of putting a fucking sword right through his fucking heart, which I thought I'd done before, I actually got on top of his body, opened the cunt up and just put my hand in there and fucking ripped his heart out.

Of course, I smelt the fucking morbid, horrible, farty colon flesh of that dragon as I pulled its heart out – 'Fucking have that!' It was kind of weird, because as I pulled the heart out, the dragon's chest started to deflate – like a fucking bouncy castle. Then, just to be sure, I had to sit and watch this fucker go cold to make sure he was well and truly fucking dead . . . I watched him turn from that macabre green rainbow-trouty looking thing to an actual fucking marble-slab cold bastard. Yeah, he's gone from green to grey to marble. He's sinking. He's gone.

Then I thought, 'You know what? Don't celebrate his death too much; just get the fuck out of there.' And I was right, because after a while, of course, he did come back, but he only came back as small baby dragons.

Now those babies can be really naughty little fuckers – what they do is kind of rub the back of your leg, and the moment you look back over your shoulder they come flying at you and you've got no option but to sever their heads with a single swoop of your blade. Another one kept going, 'Come on! Come on!' and blowing this little puff of flame from his mouth, almost like a smoke ring. Nothing big, just enough to let you know he was there – 'What's that in the dim light? Oh, it's that baby dragon.' And he called me over, and he was like, 'I know you, because you kind of killed my dad, but I just want to talk to you,' and I'm like, 'Yeah, I want to talk to you, too, let me get real close.' So when he got real close to me, I just fucking served him with a rather blunt instrument. I served him up, proper stitched him, and then threw his body to the floor.

I had a few of those moments, because those dragons – the baby ones – they come at you fast. I should probably make clear at this point that these are metaphorical dragons, not real ones. I'm not on acid.

Whether it's a particular situation, or a place, or a person that's trying to drag you back in, they're all baby dragons to me. After getting so clean while I was making the album, having *The Journey Man* finished is obviously another one of those naughty little fuckers waiting to try its luck. That's why I need to make sure I keep busy doing the right kind of things. Because I'm a little bit insatiable. I've got a lot of energy – certainly more than most, even as old as I am now – and if I don't channel it in good directions, it'll find another way to come out.

That's why I'm thinking of trying some type of meditation, to keep the baby dragons at bay. I wonder if sitting in a room doing fuck all apart from playing Xbox can be meditation? Or how about sitting in a room wanking very slowly? I hope so, because I think both of those meditational practices would definitely suit me.

E5. The Music of Chance

Where am I? I'm in St Martin's Lane, in London's old theatre district. It's four in the morning in early March 2017, and I've come to England for four weeks to start the whole promotional campaign for my new album. I've just been in the shower – not a nice sight to see, me in the shower. Let's have a timeout for a second while I apply a bit of deodorant. Lucky for you this book does not link to video.

Except it kind of does. Because I was just talking to Lyle Lindgren. He's a kid I've been sort of mentoring for a while now, who ended up helping me make the videos for the first two tracks from the album. It's wrong to talk about someone being 'the son you never had' when you have had sons of your own you've kind of failed with. But I guess it's one of the ironies of life that sometimes it's easier to be paternal towards people you aren't actually related to. That's something I often find myself thinking when I'm doing lectures or presentations and talking to all these young kids who, inevitably in that situation, are almost looking up to me. So you become this kind of father figure for other people, however much you might not have succeeded in being that for some of your own kids.

In a way, that's what the story of these two videos is all about – me trying to do a better job of parenting now than I was able to do in the past. When I first met Lyle he was working for a popular kids' TV channel. He came to film at my house, and I liked him from day one. He was really fascinated by gold teeth, and I just thought, 'This kid's got some spunk,' so I took him under my wing. I ended up flying him to New York with me a couple of times – he was running round the Bronx with this fucking massive camera and I guess he reminded me of myself at that age in the way he really wanted to understand the culture and seemed willing to put the work in and try to absorb everything around him. Also, looking back, I guess it was not long after I went on my first trip to New York that I was looking for my own father and finding him and not finding him at the same time. So maybe that brought the idea of fatherhood to mind.

Anyway, the first video we made was for 'I Adore You', which is a song with a story that goes back a few years and in a way explains how I ended up moving to Thailand and making the album there. My daughter, Chance, was fourteen at the time and I was taking her to school in Hertfordshire in England. She got in the car, but I'd forgotten something, so I went back in the house and was rummaging around looking for it, then when I came back out from the house Chance was crying. I asked her what was the matter, and she showed me her old iPod with the wheel on the front of it, and the name of the track on the screen said 'I Adore You'.

She said, 'This track's beautiful, it's amazing,' but I replied, 'That's not finished, I left it.' I'd spent some time working on that track in the studio with Jim Heist, but while the music side of it was fantastic, the beats weren't quite doing it for me. As an alchemist, you've got to do it right! I was at the tail-end of my divorce at the time, and I was in two minds about what I wanted to do next. I was in deep with Mika by then and kind of thinking, 'I just don't want to be in England any more.' So I told Chance, 'I can always finish it,' and then when I started working with James of Ulterior Motive – who is a fucking genius, by the way – I told him, 'Look, I'm going to start this fucking album, this could be the first track. In fact, you guys are on fire right now, why don't you just do the drums?'

So he did it. Job done, and it was brilliant, and that sent all these other ideas spinning around in my head: 'You know what? I'm going to move to Thailand. We're going to sell this fucking house. That means the studio's going to be shut down, all this other stuff, but we'll ride that out.' And lo and behold – the manifestation of positive fucking thinking – all of a sudden we've got this studio in Thailand, and I'm going to make an album. Fast forward a couple more years – it's five altogether, as Chance is nineteen now. The album's done, and I've flown back into London to DJ at the Boiler Room. It's a nineties set they want because apparently everyone's celebrating nineties rave culture now – it's about fucking time! Sasha's playing, I'm playing, we destroy that, then I go straight on to the video shoot.

Now Lyle's doing the video, and he's really bringing a new strength to it. I've pulled in a few favours, and I've got one of my really, really good friends from way back to play the lead. It's the actor Stephen Graham, who was in *Boardwalk Empire*, *Pirates of the Caribbean*, all this other stuff – he's just done the Tom Hardy series, *Taboo*, which is wicked. He's a brilliant man – a *savant* – who totally embodies what the whole *Journey Man* thing stands for. I don't mean it in the dictionary sense, where it's one word and means someone who's quite professional at doing something in a worn-down kind of way. In fact, it's more like the opposite of that – journey men, journey *people*, as it's women too, but that wouldn't sound so good as a title – who have gone on these great journeys and lost everything and then come back.

Stephen has suffered with a few demons, as I did, but you can see from his performance the way he's projecting it into his acting – it's like all of that pain is channelled now. It's the same thing with me and my music, organising the chaos into something that makes sense, so this sound is all of my emotions translated into another medium. I do almost think of the music as a piece

142   **ALL THINGS REMEMBERED**

of cinematography, because in my head it feels like I'm getting things down on celluloid as much as via a digital recording.

So it's a two-day shoot, and Stephen just owns it. We do a lot of the filming at the old Deptford police station, next to where they used to make *The Bill*. The basic storyline is that Lyle's daughter plays a young Chance at five, and it's all about the separation of the father and the daughter, but there's a real triangulation in this, because it also represents my son, Jamie, who's doing a life sentence in prison. And Stephen Graham being in prison also represents me, ironically not being in prison at the peak of my career in the nineties (although plenty of people thought I should be) but still being incarcerated in a jail of my own making – drugs, rock 'n' roll, everything else – to the point of rejecting my own kids.

The energy I'm putting into this kid Lyle is a great investment because I'm already getting it back. Lloyds wouldn't give me that return, and neither would Barclays. Lyle does a great job and he's adapted very well, and I think he's going to go on to great heights. The other video we're going to do together, which is the second of this kind of trilogy, is for 'Castaway'. What this track represents for me is what New York smelt like when I first went there in '84 – the brake dust from the subway, the scent of a seventy-five-cent pizza, hearing Prince singing 'Kiss' on the radio for the first time – but the way we're going to represent that in the video, because it is kind of the same feeling, is by the idea of being a castaway on this ridiculously beautiful island in southern Thailand.

There's this long, tall boat cutting through the beautiful blue water, and the camera's going to start out really close to the water, like one of those *Predator*-type movies which kicks off with the helicopter – then the drone lifts up and up before it comes to a halt above these five Buddhist monks in the boat. We cut to the interior of the boat, and we see these five monks with these individual wrought-iron keys that they're turning over in their hands. You can see the age of their hands, and the creases on their faces, but there's no particular expression in their eyes, they're just looking at the shoreline of the island approaching.

We cut to a beautiful woman on the beach, her hands down by her sides, the water dripping off her fingers. She holds one hand up to her head to shade herself from the sun, and is looking curiously out towards the sea. Then she turns and carries on walking down the beach, and we cut to the drone moving across these beautiful mountains, then it comes to a kind of Joshua tree halfway up, and there's a slight oddity about that in the middle of nowhere. The shot cuts back first to the girl and then the boat and the monks, and then to these children's footprints in the sand, which the drone is following. Then it cuts back to the boat again, but this time it's the girl there, not the monks, and she's holding something close to her chest, but we can't see what it is. Then we cut back to the footprints and the mountains and we see the woman on the beach opening her eyes, and realise it was a dream state. Then the boat hits the shoreline further down the beach, and we see the monks' orange robes draping into the water, with their feet beneath, as they disembark.

As the monks walk towards her up the beach, the woman falls to her knees and puts her head to the sand. Black screen. Then she opens her eyes and the monks have thrown her a full set of jailer's keys – all the original keys now put together on one ring – down onto the sand. The camera looks over her shoulder, and we see the monks walking off into the distance, as if they'd never stopped. She picks up the keys in jubilation and runs down the beach – we see her feet, then it cuts to the kids' footprints, then all of a sudden the shot opens up and we catch up to these little kids running, with the drone capturing their movement.

ALL THINGS REMEMBERED

We see the excitement on the faces of all these different kids from Koko's class at school in Thailand – Thai kids, half-Japanese kids, my daughter. They keep on running until they come upon a grand piano – a beautiful old Steinway, but it's knackered – turned over on its back, half in the water, half on the beach, with the waves lapping over it. It's just like me finding the scrap car – the old burnt-out Austin Allegro or Mk 1 Ford Escort – when I was a kid, except they've found this broken-down piano. They climb on top of it and they're jumping down and splashing in the water. Then the beautiful woman catches up with them. She holds her arms out and one of the kids runs towards her, then she's spinning them around, lost in the joy of this moment. Then she kind of pulls back. The drone starts doing 360s around the piano and takes one step towards the sea, and we cut to a distant shot of the monks' boat. She's already dropped the keys into the water by the shore, when she picked up the first kid who ran towards her, and we get a close-up of the waves lapping over the wrought-iron keys alongside the piano and the kids and the fun, as she kind of leaves them to it.

Now she's on the shoreline, holding something close to her chest with both hands, tying in with the earlier shot on the boat, when she was clutching the self-same thing with her eyes closed. Now she opens her hands and you can see she's holding some broken piano keys – two black and two white. Then we cut back to the shot we had at the beginning, from the drone crossing the sea, but now we see these piano keys, just floating in the water. Then slowly the drone starts to rise – no faster than 5 m.p.h. – and we see the whole piano floating in the sea. The drone continues to rise until we see all of this beautiful marine-blue coral beneath the water, with the piano just floating out to sea above it.

Where am I? In my imagination, that's where. This is the storyboard of the film that depicts the freedom that Thailand has

given me – the harmony between the mountains that I've climbed all my life and the keys I now have to unlock my potential, in the same way that we can unlock the potential of those children. It's going to be the first video I've ever actually directed. The black notes of the broken piano that the children are dancing on represent the destructive elements of my own past life, which are also part of the music. In the same way, 'I Adore You' is about the lost love between a father and a daughter, a son and a father, while at the same time it's about finding something new.

ALL THINGS REMEMBERED

Everyone needs a home. Especially when you're displaced and the beautiful model of that nuclear family with the perfect rosy driveway has fallen apart – that's when having a place where people know you and you know them is pretty fucking essential. My label Metalheadz has been that place for me since 1994, when I started it with Kemi and Storm.

Because I was on this kind of *Terminator* mission at that time, where I'd been programmed by my two Miyagis Marc and Dego (I know that's a different film, but you get the picture), I analyse the things I was doing back then almost as the actions of an AI. The circuitry was definitely taking me in the right direction with Metalheadz, and the humanity of the collective brain within the steely exo-skull of that logo could never be denied.

It was like I'd created a new Lew Joseph or Hammerwich home, but this time full of the right kids. Hey, don't call me Fagin – I wasn't going to be putting little children through tiny holes in windows to bring me back the stuff that was shiny in the house. But I wanted them to bring me the sound back. 'Give me your interpretation of what falling between the black notes and the white notes really is' – that's what Metalheadz has always been to me.

Once you've been granted the freedom of Headzville, you're not going to want to live anywhere else. There aren't many electronic labels which are still reinventing themselves more than twenty years down the line – allowing the old guard like Doc Scott and Digital, who've been around since the beginning, to keep on growing, at the same time as bringing through new

people, like SP 81 from my old home town, Wolverhampton.

I think it was just a question of us hanging in there till the next generation came through, although for a while back there it was anything but a foregone conclusion that Metalheadz would be on the up and up again in 2017. From 2001 to 2006, for instance, we weren't really the name on anyone's lips. And a lot of the credit for the fact that eleven years further on we're going stronger than ever goes to Anthony Crook, my label-head (and how can you not trust someone with that surname?).

Anthony lives up north, right opposite where they make *Emmerdale Farm*, which is a funny place for such a hardcore, headstrong raver to come from. I first became friends with him four or five years ago, after he was on a Hidden Agenda record we released. He also used to run a label called Dispatch, but you'd know Metalheadz was the label closest to his heart even if you hadn't seen the wicked tattoo of the logo he's got on his chest. I didn't know he had that till the time I caught a glimpse of it out of the corner of my eye when he came back from kick-boxing training – he's bearing the fucking mark, mate. You just don't get that commitment at EMI.

I love Anthony like a chubby little brother – hence the kick-boxing. It's like *Fat Fighters* for aggressive people: he loses weight and it keeps him chilled. He was the one who gave me the kick up the arse I needed by saying, 'Look, man, you can't throw in the towel – you've had an amazing innings with the first hundred Metalheadz releases, but let's take it to another hundred.' That was why I changed the letters at the start of the catalogue number from 'meth' to 'meta' when we passed that milestone – to show it was a new start. At the time of writing we're sixty-eight into that second century, and I think we've released a greater quality of music in the last two years than we had done in the previous ten.

The crew mentality is something that's always been important to me – from street-hockey to breakdancing to the Tats Cru on the New York subways. That was what kept us going through the lean times when no one really wanted to know, and that's what's given us the momentum to experience an amazing rebirth over the last couple of years. It's not about restricting people's freedom as individuals, but encouraging them to express themselves within a collective ethos. 'No man is an island' – that's probably the best way of summing it up, although you could also say that our Death Star is finally complete.

SIDE F

F1. Why Coming Home Smelling of Kebabs Is a Bad Idea When You Own a Boa Constrictor

I always wanted a snake. It was a Miami thing, from when I was working the flea markets. You'd see a lot of drug dealers, players and hustlers walking round the markets, wearing boa constrictors like scarves. It was all about status. Anyone can wear snakeskin shoes – all you've got to do is have the money – but if you've got a live one around your neck, everyone knows you're a real player. 'What the fuck? It's a black guy with a boa constrictor . . .' That's fucking balling!

There was this one guy called Russell who had one and he let me feel the texture of its skin. It was beautiful, like something out of *Blade Runner* – 'Is this synthetic? No, it's real . . .' And from that point on, I was fascinated by them, so ultimately I got one. I didn't have to go far to get it, either. It was when I was living in Bovingdon, in Hertfordshire, of all places. There was a mad little exotic pet shop on the high street: tarantulas, meerkats, they had the lot. Including this boa constrictor which I bought and named Lanny. It was manageable at first, but it just kept getting bigger and bigger. And the question of what do you fucking do with this giant motherfucker started to get more urgent, especially once he'd learned to let himself out of his glass tank – the lock would come off and Lanny would lean his huge body against it and push it open.

He'd taken a particular liking to motorbikes, and his favourite thing to do was wrap himself round my Ducati. But sometimes he'd leave the garage and go for a bit of a wander. That was when you had to watch him. He'd done this thing a couple of times before where he'd stand up in front of me and hiss so I'd feel his breath. You'd think, 'Shit, Lanny,' but then you'd step back and he'd get down and be all right. You could just go, 'Come on, mate,' and touch his nose and he'd back away, then you could just pick him up and put him back in his tank. But on this one occasion when I'd come back from having a greasy kebab after a night out – Crystal Kebabs, Holloway Road, delicious – it was half an hour's drive home but I obviously still smelled like dinner.

I'd had a few jars, and maybe I was a little complacent. I open the door, he backs away, then I go to pick him up by his underside. There's a hissing sound and then he strikes. He's wrapped around my arm. All of a sudden, I'm in a fight. Do you know how powerful a 15-foot-long boa constrictor is once it has turned on you? Strong as fuck. Lanny's got a full-on latch, and he's definitely getting the better of my arm.

At this point, my pal runs in from the car. Luckily, I've been doing some wallpapering, so the table's still out with a special pair of wallpaper scissors on it. He grabs them, and I tell him, 'Right, let's put them in between his fucking jaws and lever him off.' So that's what we do, but it takes a while, and as Lanny is finally prised away, there's claret everywhere from the wound to my arm – the angle of his jaw's got to be 120 degrees at least, and once I was finally free my arm looked like a deflated old leather casey football.

I wasn't angry with Lanny. It was my fault for not securing him properly and then coming home a bit pissed and smelling of meat. But that's the point when you realise, 'He's got to go.' It could've been my daughter in those jaws, or my dog – my mastiff at the time would probably have put up a pretty good fight, if he hadn't had cancer, but with a kid you've got to be careful. So I gave Lanny to Whipsnade Zoo and off he went.

I've still got the scars on my arm to remember him by. If you were here now I'd point to them and say, 'That's where the cunt got me.' It'd be emotional. I don't know how big Lanny is now – probably colossal – but it was great having him for a while. I loved watching him feed. You didn't have to give him live mice, he would take dead ones, but you could kind of entice him when you handed them over. The other fascinating thing was the shedding of the skin. He'd do it all the time – even more often than David Bowie – and the old ones he'd get shot of were like the papery bit between the layers of an onion. I visualise the fabric of my life as being like that stuff – what's left when you cut down through the layers – so watching the skin-shedding process unfold in my own home was fascinating for me.

I realise that the whole 'attacked by your own boa constrictor' thing is a bit ridiculous, but it's almost like I've got some kind of regressive pimp gene that can't help but come out sometimes. My wife and I laugh about it.

There was a funny time in China when I got myself a suit made. In Hong Kong there's a famous tailor called Sam – you can take any suit to him you want, and he will make you a copy. They had people that do the same thing in Shanghai, and I'd found this piece of material from a five-inch colour swatch that I wanted made up into a suit. This was on my second or third visit to see Mika, when she was still working in Shanghai – before she moved back to Montreal for a year and I bombarded her with letters before finally popping the question, after which she came to England. I was out exploring Shanghai when she was at work. She'd told me where to find this place that made suits, and I was very definite about the fabric I liked – 'I want one like that; in fact, I want two.'

Mika came with me to collect them. The woman pulled out the fucking suits, and my missus, she couldn't stop laughing.

I'm like, 'Jesus Christ, I've definitely got that regressive pimp gene.' This suit was a three-piece, and it was like a fucking NBA draft suit – you know, when the basketball players get signed up, and they all wear that horrible suit? The reason it was horrible in this case was because it was plaid. The five-inch swatch looked all right, but blown up to man-size it was more like a cloth I'd put on my dining table.

My missus-to-be was going, 'Oh my God, look at you!' And what I saw in the mirror reminded me of the picture of my dad that my mum had on her mantelpiece – the only picture I knew of him, growing up. He's there with his foot on a log, with a bald head, wearing a really bad plaid suit with some really bad crocodile shoes against this really bad sepia background. When he met me at the airport in Miami I saw him for the first time since I was a baby – I knew it was him straight away – and thought, 'Oh shit, I'm going to go bald – that's what I'm going to look like.' And now, with a little bit of help from that suit, this prophecy had come true: I'd finally become my father.

F2. Rage

The time I spent in Miami was a massive eye-opener, but for a while when I came back to England things just didn't feel right. I almost felt like I'd been displaced, as if I'd lost a sense of where I belonged and what I was meant to be doing. But then I met Kemi . . .

My fellow West Midlander, Valerie Olukemi A. Olusanya – Kemi for short – would be the heart and soul of my label Metalheadz. And as one half of Kemistry and Storm she'd inspire some of the biggest tunes of the first wave of drum 'n' bass. To put the sad ending of the story right at the front for anyone who doesn't know it, Kemi died tragically in a freak accident in 1999, when the steel body of a dislodged cat's eye was thrown up by a van in front of her on the M3, flew through the windscreen of the car she was in and killed her instantly. It's how alive she was when I knew her that I prefer to remember, though. And Kemi always said she wanted to die young, so we got a lot of peace out of that.

She took my breath away when I first met her – long blonde dreadlocks, worked in Red or Dead. I'd done New York. I'd done Miami. I wanted to go out. I wanted to hook up – 'Let's go to a club and rave.' I went down to Rage at Heaven on a Thursday night three weeks running and couldn't get in. The guy who stopped me on the door – Paul Churchill – became a good friend later on and we laugh about this now.

Once I finally got inside, it was like a whole other world. I soon realised that standing around trying to impersonate a New York gangster (which was what I was doing at the time) wasn't the right look. There were people on podiums with their clothes off, hanging from the rafters. And there's me, Bronx Bob, sweating like a rapist in my full length goose-down. Rage was a different thing: laser on one side, silhouette of a DJ, an atmosphere that was second to none, and music that wasn't charged with rap culture but with the emotionally loaded angst of what the underground of this country was really feeling.

In terms of the rave scene, whatever was happening at Rage had definitely come out of the fields, and was now running parallel to the outdoor events that were still going on – Donnington, World Dance at Lydd airport . . . I got into those too, but because my starting point was different, that maybe set up a parallax in terms of how I viewed (or heard) them. But that was a good thing, because it gave me a different angle. When 'Terminator' got done, I called Grooverider from John Truelove's studio in Arlington Road, Camden, and said, 'I've made something, I think it's going to change the music.'

I'd got to know Grooverider from going to the record shop Music Power in Green Lanes. It's not there any more (it was an estate agent's last time I heard, which says it all as far as gentrification is concerned), but in those days it was *the* place. Me, Kemi and Storm would stand there and wait to get a glimpse of Grooverider coming in on a Thursday – or a Friday, you had to go both days, because you didn't know what day he was going to turn up. We'd wait for an age. Then his car would come round the back, you'd see him come in, he'd grab a whole bunch of records, Chris Power, the co-owner, would play them to him very quickly, and he'd take some and leave others. You'd think about what he'd taken, because you'd want to try to get a copy – if there was an extra one, or maybe order one for a week later – log the tunes, write them down, get what you could, then go back and listen to the music. That was how we learned – we did our homework.

My favourite fishing boat

Kamala Bay

At work in my studio in Thailand

With Ice-T and Cliff Whyte on the set of *CSI*

Stussy canvas. This was a very early piece for them . . . and me
(painted with Sarah Gregory)

The Bronx's finest

From my *Lost Tribes* exhibition

With Ken Swift of the Rock Steady Crew and Birdie in Riverside Park, New York

Love and Heart, a Thai graffiti collaboration with Bio – Tats Kru

Metalheadz gold disc for *Timeless*. We broke the mould

Tank Girl test 1. New work for a show in
Phuket in 2018

Three abstracts

Sea of James, either just before or just after
chi kung

Yoga fashion on point

I'd loved the rave thing from the very beginning. It was happening before I went to Miami, but by the time I got back it had all got a little bit too saccharine for me. It felt like running into a sweet shop: 'OK, I've dropped a few pills, done whatever.' Fair enough but, you know, what's next? I just felt that it needed something else, and I think that's when the B-boy switch well and truly flicked for me. I guess it switched for the government in a different way, which was where the 1994 Criminal Justice Act would come in. So for me the darker vibe that came into the more breakbeat-oriented tunes in the early nineties was also about signifying darker times for this country. That's definitely where my tracks like 'Sinister' and 'Dark Rider' came in – they were all about the other side of what was going on.

I think the sense of displacement that I'd felt on coming back from America aligned with the gap which had opened up in British music. Because before that you'd had the rave scene going down the Judge Jules route, and then on the more soulful side of it you'd had Soul II Soul, which I'd had a personal link with through knowing Nellee Hooper from the whole Bristol connection. Even though the disparity between these two things was huge, I had a foot in both camps.

People often forget now what a big deal Soul II Soul were, but when they first blew up they were massive. Especially Jazzie B. Then the whole shop thing happening took it all to another level, not least on the business side, as a black British musical phenomenon that seemed to be in the mainstream on its own terms, rather than in a way that a record company dictated. I got to meet Jazzie a few times, and did some merchandise for him, because I was designing t-shirts at the time.

When I was living with Gus Coral in Swiss Cottage I even sat in on sessions at Mayfair Studios and Utopia in Primrose Hill, where Soul II Soul were doing 'A Dream's a Dream' with

Howie Bernstein (better known as Howie B), who I love dearly to this day. Me and Howie got really close then, and this was hip-hop production done really well on home turf, which was very inspiring to me. I remember being in there looking at this studio, listening to this music coming out of it that was Soul II Soul and thinking, 'Wow.' But even at that time I was always flipping back to the underground. A few years later, when I had a 12-inch single of 'Terminator' I saw Jazzie in his Mercedes and handed it to him. He said, 'Cheers, kid,' and drove off. I don't know if he ever listened to it.

The first time I met Marc and Dego they were onstage at the Astoria, as Manix, along with two kids from Nottingham called Nebula II. When I saw that, coming off the back of Rage, it was exactly the affirmation that I'd been waiting for, because this was breakbeat – 'Oh my God, the helium rave's stopped!' To be fair, they still had a trace element of helium, because Marc would always do a little bit of hands in the air, but the underlying breakbeat aspect of that music was undeniable.

Things could've gone a few different ways around this time – The Prodigy were starting to happen and there were other things going on. But then Grooverider dropped 'Straight Outta Hell' in 1992 and it was game over. Thank you very much, Raymond. I could never have stayed happy in helium once I'd heard that.

The way Marc and Dego and Ian ran Reinforced Records – the label that released the music which was made in their Dollis Hill studio – it was impossible not to get caught up in it. People are making music now when they're fourteen, and they're doing all this unbelievable stuff – especially in grime – but I never made a record till I was twenty-seven. I was a late starter. People forget that. Maybe partly because I had some lost time to make up for, but once I was doing it, I was doing it. We were hands-on then. I think the first 12-inch record I ever made – Ajax Project

– the sleeve was potato-printed. I did it with Aggi, a guy from Iceland who's sadly no longer with us.

Everything was DIY in those days. You'd drive around, go to record shops – it didn't matter if they were in Hertfordshire. When they owed you money, you'd get the money. If they didn't have the money, you'd take the till! It was literally like that. It was a little bit cowboy back then, and you could hear that in the music. When I listen back to tracks from those days now I think, 'You eclectic maniac!' But I also blame the wonderful, wonderful craft of hip-hop, and the impression that it made on me – having never previously left this country – on being catapulted into New York at the age of eighteen, when my mind was wide open to the smell of the brake dust from the subway trains. That stuff crept in there and it's never fully come out. I hope it never does.

Next up after Dollis Hill was Synthetic Records at Arlington Road. I think the label itself was created by one of Echo and the Bunnymen, but I never knew which one. That was where Diane Charlemagne from the Manchester funk band 52nd Street became involved. I asked her manager John Noel – who was Howie's manager at the time and would end up being Russell Brand's manager years later – if he had any singers, and he told me, 'I've got this wonderful young lady called Diane Charlemagne.' He was right. Diane – who is also sadly no longer with us, having died of kidney cancer in 2015 – was indeed a wonderful young lady. I'd loved some of 52nd Street's records, so I sent her some ideas and we started working together.

'Kemistry' was the first thing we did together, and then 'Angel'. 'Kemistry' was the hardest to do because at that point I didn't know what songwriting was – all I really knew was breakbeats. But I'd had good teachers in Marc and Dego, and also Howie B, who'd taught me that making records is simply about setting up your environment, bringing in the different elements – whether it's samples, musicians or singers – and then putting the whole thing together. I was pulling away from Marc and Dego by then in terms of being in the studio, because I wanted to do my own thing.

Even most of my first two Synthetic EPs had been done without them. I'd said to Reinforced, 'Look, guys, I've got a chance here to break out of the car boot, man; I've got a chance to get out of the van,' which is what we'd always talked about in terms of driving round selling our own records. Marc said to me, 'Oh, you're going to have to hire another sampler.' So we got another sampler in, and it was like, 'Reinforced are working on 900s, I've got 1000s.' Me and a guy called Linford, who was my right-hand man at that point, filled up two samplers and off we went. They were asking, 'What are you going to do with this?' I'm like, 'Don't worry about it. I'm going to arrange it.'

From very early on I had all these ideas for pieces of music. If you wanted a visual representation of the process of turning those blueprints into actual songs, graffiti would give it to you. You've got the outline in your head, so you draw your outline. At first it's two-dimensional and in black and white. So you're going to make it colour. You put the outline in a light colour, then you work back all through the shades until it gets darker and darker and darker, then finally you outline the piece and put the highlights in. That's the EQ.

For me, making music has always been a painting process – the two things are one and the same. And in the same way that a graffiti piece would have to survive the elements, so music would have to make the transition into a club or outdoor rave environment. We'd make that journey too, which is something that's been a special part of my life. Many a rave we'd go to . . . You're on the way home and the battery's gone or you've run out of petrol. So you're sat by the side of the road, freezing your tits off, thinking, 'How the fuck are we going to get back?' Thumb a lift from other ravers. That's the answer.

I remember World Dance at Lydd airport – a massive night, God bless my main man Jay Pender for making that happen: legend! I'm there with Randall, who was the DJ I probably travelled around with most. I was always carrying his record box into Orange on a Saturday night – me and our mate Marlon where his designated box-boys. Anyway, we were in this guy called Monkey's BMW on the way back from Lydd – I remember we had the dubs of 'Menace' (which I did as the Rufige Kru) with us for the first time – when we hit a traffic island. Car went sideways – up in the air – lands – it's a write-off. Somehow we got out. We were very lucky that we actually had our seatbelts on in the back – I don't know why we put them on, but we did. The person who wasn't lucky was Monkey, who was basically testing the car for us because Randall was going to buy it off him the next day.

So there was a distraught Monkey flinging his arms around in distress as he looked at his write-off, whereas I'm thinking, 'Oh my God, man, Randall – I can't believe we're alive . . . but we've got to get to Paradise' – not the afterlife, the club in Islington, because Randall was playing the last set.

Jay Pender's Paradise Club – our second coming – would turn into one of our main stomping grounds for the next few years, and getting back there on time was all that mattered to us that night. We somehow managed to thumb a lift, and GQ was on the mic when we finally turned up. Seeing him was such a blessing – it made us feel more alive than any E we'd ever taken. 'GQ, you ain't going to believe what's happened . . .' 'Tell me, tell me, let Randall get on.' Randall gets on, and it's like, 'We just survived a car crash' – that's how important it was for us. Get to the rave, get to the gig, play the gig, see daylight on your way out.

Once I was doing stuff in the studio, I missed a few gigs and

Randall left me a message. It's on the beginning of 'This Is a Bad' on *Timeless*, and it says, 'So, man, pick up the phone, man . . . you'll not pick up the phone, man, you're rubbish, man,' and he just coats me. It's an answerphone message and it's a beautiful thing because between the lines what it's really about is how special it feels to be driving back to the city when everyone else is asleep. This ain't Santa, this is going to the rave. This is culture. This is where we've got to be: M6, man, M1, bam, let's get there, Manchester, Birmingham, Sheffield, bam, get back, Leeds, get back to London, get back home, get to Paradise. Get to Paradise Club, it's important.

By the time I was doing *Timeless* I was driving up the A1 from Gus's place in Swiss Cottage to Rob Playford's studio in his semi-detached house in Stevenage every day. That physical motion and the tiredness and exhilaration of it fed back into the music, too. At one point, when I was under the mixing desk working on 'Inner City Life', we'd got to twelve minutes in and I thought, 'I'm going to push this.' I started doing some really experimental stuff by scrolling the wheel of the Akai sampler, which as far as I knew (and know) was something that hadn't been done before.

That scrolling across the wheel is the snaking sound that you hear in *Timeless*. To me that's what inner-city life was all about in reality as well as in song form – the pressure and the velocity pushing you into new shapes. Even though this song came later – on the album he made as E-Dancer – I always think of Kevin Saunderson's track 'Velocity Funk' in this connection. Kevin is a good example of someone who has successfully crossed in and out of the mainstream. He was one of the 'Belleville Three' – with Juan Atkins and Derrick May – who were pioneers of Detroit techno, and he also had huge worldwide pop hits as one half of Inner City with Paris Grey. Kevin's music has had a huge influence on my life.

Once word started to get around about *Timeless,* a lot of music-industry people suddenly came out of the woodwork. Pete Tong was on the radar, Clive Black . . . All of a sudden people wanted me in their offices. Not everyone got it, though. I handed the A&R man at A&M the cassette – because this was before everything was on CD or download – and asked him to turn it over when the side finished. He was sitting there, only ten minutes or so into 'Inner City Life', when his eyes started rolling – 'I want to go for lunch anyway, but listen, yeah, it sounds great, cool, wicked . . . I'll be in touch.' I'm like, 'You know what? It ain't going with you, mate.'

It wasn't long before Pete Tong had signed us up and the record had gone to number seven in the album charts (which still meant something in those days; in fact, it meant a lot) and was winning two awards at the first MOBOs in 1996. One was for best jungle act, but the other was for best overall album – up against George Michael, Destiny's Child, Mark Morrison . . . Go figure, people. The exciting thing was, this was underground drum 'n' bass music, and we hadn't had to water it down at all. What we'd actually done was jazz it up.

F3. *Goldie's Band – By Royal Appointment*

Goldie's Band was a three-part BBC TV show I made in 2011, where me and some music-industry people got a bunch of talented kids together and coached them to do a performance at Buckingham Palace. I know that looks a bit mad written down, but it did actually happen – you can still see me on YouTube, wearing a bow tie and sitting next to Prince Harry in the audience at the palace, while Natalie Duncan does an amazing version of her song 'Princess Adrina'.

A lot of good things came out of that show, but Natalie was – and is – the best of them. She was a young girl from Nottingham who is undoubtedly one of the most gifted singers and songwriters and pianists I've ever worked with. But she's also very sensitive – in the same way that I am. Even more so, in some ways, because she sees dead people, like the kid in *The Sixth Sense*. Guy Chambers, one of the mentors on the show, went to see her, I think with Miss Dynamite, and they sent me the video of the session back. Natalie actually stopped them in the middle of the session and said, 'Someone else is sitting there.' This person visits her all the time, and she was fucking freaking out. I knew then that she was a fucking star.

Unfortunately there was a bit of a fuck-up with the old due diligence in the aftermath of that show. This was not fucking *X Factor*, guys, this was not a small viola playing, cut to parents, cut to close-up of parents, cut to young girl crying, cut to fade-out, bring music up. This was not that kind of fucking show. But still, mistakes were made. You should not pick up someone precious like Natalie, sign her to a fucking major and get her a flat in the middle of Ladbroke Grove. Great thinking. Round of a-fucking-pplause, mate. She didn't get looked after in the way that she needed to be, the whole thing fucking imploded and she ended up having to go back to her parents' and spend a few years kind of in the mire.

Fast forward to a couple of years ago, just after I'd moved to Thailand, and I woke up one morning at the back end of a dream, thinking, 'I've got to reach out to this girl.' So I phoned her up and told her, 'Natalie, I've written something for you.' It was kind of a classical piece based around four chords called 'The Ballad Celeste', and I honestly think it's one of the most beautiful songs I've ever written. It's like a broken nursery rhyme for adults, taking words from everywhere – from *Alice in Wonderland* to the headless horseman in *Sleepy Hollow* – and it resonated with her. She sent me back a demo, saying, 'I don't think this is any good, but have a listen,' and when I put it on in the car it was so incredible I just pulled over to the side of the road and cried like a baby.

Natalie's in a much better place now – she's been living in St Albans – and she contributed three wonderful pieces to *The Journey Man*. For as long as we're both making music, that woman will always have me in her life, because she's just phenomenal. And working with her the second time around has been all the sweeter for the fact that we've both been down that road where we kind of lost everything in different ways, but then we came back from hell, and now the clarity of our understanding is beautiful. She's like my window to the notes.

Kwabena – Kwabs for short – was another of the talented kids we had on that show, but what happened with him was a different story. In one way he's doing really well, but in another he kind of fucked up, too. I wrote the song 'Broken Man' for him, but he never came back to finish it. I presumed this was because his manager told him not to because he'd have a better chance of getting an album deal without me involved. I thought that was really poor, after I'd set up such a good platform for him. *Goldie's Band* put a big light on those guys. They were always going to be stars, but the one thing I've realised about what we do is that you should always pay respect to people that have helped you out. Don't listen to the management, finish the fucking record.

I was watching José James – another great singer, who was introduced to me by Gilles Peterson – playing at Ronnie Scott's one time not long ago when Kwabena rolled in. He saw me there and said, 'Yo, my man Goldie's here, legend in the game,' and I thought, that's my note to self. I got up, walked over to him and said, 'Kwabena – Kwabs – I love you and good luck with your success. You're doing really well, but you should have finished that fucking record. If there's one thing I've learned about this business, it's that if hindsight was in fucking cans in Waitrose, the shelves would be empty, the shelves would be fucking empty. And you did me wrong on that, we should have finished the record.'

He just kind of muttered back, 'I'm sorry . . .' I get it. You can look sheepish and I know you're a vocal powerhouse and the new album's happening and everything. But don't forget the platform that you had. That's the biggest mistake we can make when we're coming up in this game. That's why I always try to pay total respect to my peers. I don't care if they're fucking winos, or addicts, or whatever, they're still my fucking peers.

F4. Dyslexia vs Synaesthesia – Old Skool Rave Soundclash

I've always been dyslexic, which has obviously been a problem for me, but I think the way that the mind has to adapt to that situation can also open up a lot of doors. I definitely think my synaesthesia is related to it. Synaesthesia is the tendency – or the ability, depending on how you look at it – to kind of swap between the senses, and I think it's something a lot of dyslexic people seem to be able to tune into a bit more. For me it comes down to the fact that I've always seen music as colours, with basses maybe translating to dark blues, and trebles as yellows and ochres and a general sense of lights coming through.

I think that ability to visualise sound has been very helpful to me in my art as well as my music. How this colour is going to affect the one next to it is a question that will decide the nature of your composition in music as well as in painting. Sometimes you'll start with one colour, place another next to it, and then a third will confirm that the choice of the first colour was right. It's the same with instruments in a musical arrangement. And if you're seeing those two processes as overlapping from the beginning, it can't help but give you a head start in getting to grips with them both.

F5. David Bowie in Hoxton Square

Saturnz Return – my second album, which came out in 1998 – was my own personal car crash, and I didn't have a driver's air-bag. At the time I was someone who, despite all the glam and the glitz and the fantastic stuff that had happened, at three or four in the morning the cracks would appear, and the lamenting would start, and the loneliness. At that point all the drugs in the world couldn't keep it away, and the underlying reality of the situation emerged in the track 'Mother'.

I'd had a very traumatic time as a kid, and in musical terms my first way out of that had been *Timeless*. *Timeless* was the street. It was, 'I'm fucking getting on this train of music and I'm hanging on and I'm going to tell you what I feel about this life and this inner city, where I'm crying in a sea of tears and I've got my own angels.' It was all of that.

And then after the shouting and screaming stopped, it was like that thing when you're little and somebody's put their hand on your head to push you back, and you're swinging and you're swinging at them but you can't make a punch connect. You're giving it the old Charlie big-bollocks, but even as you're swinging and you're swinging, you're realising, 'You know what, man? It's not going to go away.' It was like schizophrenia, almost. It was just this sound that kept coming to me. It haunted me, night after night. Night after night. 'Leave me alone, man. I don't want to deal with it.' I could feel my mother.

That relationship was tumultuous anyway, and at the same time as making the album, the documentary *When Saturn Returnz* was being made for Channel 4. That programme had

ALL THINGS REMEMBERED

some pretty dark shit in it, even for me. The title refers – as it does with the album – to the astrological moment in your life when the planet Saturn completes its long orbit around the sun and returns to the place in the sky it held at the time of your birth. It happens for the first time when you're twenty-nine and a half years old (and the second time when you're fifty-nine, if you're lucky enough to live that long), and there's a tradition in astrology that associates this time with a huge emotional crisis. That's certainly what I was having at the time, and I was lucky enough to have a camera crew following me through it.

There's nothing I regret about that, though. The documentary was huge for me – it was my mum and my dad, all of that stuff, a very deep thing. The record I made at the time was an album that Polygram did not really want. And I can understand why the track 'Mother' in particular would not be everyone's cup of tea. It was a sixty-minute piece whose underlying message was basically, *'Argh!'* I can understand why it's a headfuck for people, but for me it was a really important part of my life, because I wanted to know who I was. I wanted to explore my abandonment issues, which are always with me.

The fact that I was at the height of my addiction to cocaine at the time – and it really was raging at this point – obviously complicated matters. And as an additional complication, it was at the time when I'd just started working on 'Mother' that I got the phone call – from Madonna herself – asking me to produce her album. She'd fallen out with someone and I was the next name in the frame, because she always liked to work with people who were happening. Even though it was a big thing for me to turn down, I'm glad I didn't go to Los Angeles to make Madonna's album, because I think the ultimate consequence would probably have been me found in a hotel room with a needle in my arm, a gun with an empty fucking magazine beside me and my brains blown out. I honestly believe that would have happened because, as an artist, I wasn't ready – I had too much shit of my own to deal with.

I think my basic mentality then was that I was trying to create as much music as possible in the hope of saving myself. 'Letter of Fate' was a good example of how this worked on a practical level. The lyrics were a suicide note (from a botched earlier attempt on my own life) which fell out of my belongings in the loft of an old house. This happened just as I was starting work on the album, and I decided it would be a great idea to say goodbye to this fucking suicide note and the weak child who wrote it. So I looked at the note and I created 'Letter of Fate', which has the sound of the tearing of a piece of paper built into the music. Destroying that note was just a way of symbolising what I felt – putting a marker down in terms of taking back my life. It didn't mean the drugs stopped. It didn't mean anything practical, really, beyond the symbolism.

At the start of the track, you hear the sound of a pen on paper, which was a bit of an avant-garde experiment and quite a traumatic thing to relive. So to heal that I obviously went off to the toilet to do some more drugs – maybe half a tab of acid and half an E. As I came back into the studio I heard this fucking voice. It sounded like a Buddhist monk. I was walking down the hallway and as I looked in the mirror I saw myself moving but my actual self seemed to stay where it was – like my physical body and my soul had separated. Obviously I was tripping out of my box. It didn't really stay there, but to me it did. Even as the sound of the voice kind of pulled me back in, I thought, 'This isn't me any more.' And in a way it wasn't. The Séancic Method was in full effect.

At any particular moment in your life, you tend to get together with people that are like-minded – both in negative and positive ways. At this point, because I was so into drugs, I obviously had a lot of drug dealers around me – that's not fucking positive, kid! But also there was the like-mindedness of working with musicians and people who understand sound, which was a much better influence. Hearing 'Letter of Fate' played back to me told me there was something else beyond me that I couldn't really fathom. Will O'Donovan, the guy who was engineering the record, seemed to get that too, because he told me, 'Look, if you put instruments inside the lid of the piano, it will create extra resonance.' I'm all about resonance, so that really spoke to me, and what it led me towards doing was the track 'Truth', which was 'Letter of Fate' backwards – from end to beginning – with instruments thrown in to mute the strings of the piano. That turned out to be a very haunting piece, which in many ways was a cry for help. It's like the physicality of a beast, some botched Frankenstein experiment like in the film *The Fly*, except the creature dies on its back with the scientist saying, 'But it was a man!'

In the middle of all this chaos, there was also David Bowie, who had been a massive influence on my early life, when I was a closet Bowie freak – 'Space Oddity' was always a different ballgame, and then there was *Low* and all the other Eno stuff, which I found out about later. After we finished *Timeless* – which Bowie had heard about through the grapevine – Pete Tong asked, 'What are you going to do next?' And I was like, 'Ah.' He mentioned something about Bowie being interested, which kind of stuck in my mind. Then I was off on an absolutely mad bender for about a week – kind of imploding with crazy stuff. One morning I woke up, in and out of delusions, and there was an envelope next to the bed with all this writing on. At first I thought it was a 'Dear John' letter – some bird's left me . . . I couldn't blame her if she had.

Then I looked down and saw that it was my writing – 'Would you lie to me lately, truth? Would you die for me lately, truth? For beast is the colour of my mood. Tomorrow for you to know that sorrow hides in sculpture.' That's a bit strong, isn't it? But still, the idea had been put in my head by Pete Tong mentioning Bowie, and he began to come through in my head – 'You lied to me lately?' – and I thought, 'Right, this thing, I want to write it for him, because his songwriting's unbelievable.'

By this time various things were happening: the deal had been signed for the new album, and we'd got the studio for Rob Playford in St Anne's Court, Soho. We'd done *Timeless* in Stevenage but now we were uptown – the advance had come through and Rob took over the lease of the studio from Mel Gaynor, the drummer in Simple Minds. Rob had his record label Moving Shadow on one floor, we'd got the studio in the back, the finance was all in place, and we were doing *Saturnz Return.* You walked in the studio and there was a huge seven-and-a-half-foot blown-up photograph of David Bowie on the wall, in his trilby, from when he'd recorded there in 1977. Almost twenty years later and he was on our radar. I expected to walk past him, but not to work with him.

Metalheadz Sunday club nights had started by then at Blue Note in Hoxton Square. There wasn't much else there, then – Shoreditch hadn't started happening as an idea yet. In a lot of ways, it was our fault. We even had board games upstairs! Yeah, sorry about that one. Anyway, it was a good idea at the time. All the big drum 'n' bass DJs and producers – Doc Scott, Photek, Fabio and Grooverider, everyone – would go there to escape some of the madness that was going on in the ragga–jungle side of things. We wanted somewhere the music-makers could listen to music and play exactly what they wanted without having to worry about the hits you'd be under pressure to play on a Friday or

Saturday. At the start it was empty – for the first few weeks there was room for me to breakdance, and this was in a small room with a low ceiling that held maybe two hundred people. Soon it started to fill up, so people would have to be down there by 7.30 to get in. I'm geeing all the DJs up by calling them and playing sixteen bars of something or other over the phone just to keep them on their toes – 'You'd better have some good shit for me on Sunday.'

Anyway, Bowie wanted to meet, so he decided to come down to Blue Note. We're sitting on the steps outside and he's rolling a cigarette, loving the place – 'You've got a great set of people in there' – feeling the influence. That's definitely where the energy came from for his drum 'n' bass reinvention with the album *Earthling*. That's what he was the master of – reinventing himself – but you always knew it was him.

So, we're sitting on the steps and all my mates are just kind of walking behind me going, 'Is that him???' 'Go away, yes, cool, chill.' Most people on the underground leave people alone: that's what they're like. Bowie comes back for a few weeks in a row and people kind of get used to him. Meanwhile I am very busy getting off my tits – doing acid, E, coke, whatever. And this thing comes to me in the night: it comes to me. I wake up, and it's there, wow, this is really good. I call David – 'Look, man, I've got this great idea—'

'Yeah, we want to make a record, a drum 'n' bass record.'

'Woah, we're not going to make a drum 'n' bass record. I want to make a ballad, Dave, I really want to make a ballad. I think a ballad would be unbelievable, because it's what wrenches me in your music – your voice.'

'Whatever, man, whatever you want to do.'

And that's how 'Truth' on *Saturnz Return* happened. If you listen to that song now you can still hear how David Bowie sang the fuck out of it.

A couple of years or so later we made a British gangster film called *Everybody Loves Sunshine* together, and when the production ran out of cash at one point, David put thirty grand of his own money in. I remember us sitting in this caravan on the Isle of Man – David's wearing a suit, and I was in a trench coat. There were some pretty serious Moss Side gangsters around on that set – some of whom are no longer with us – but I looked over at the Duke, and he was knitting. He said it chilled him out. Surreal is what I call it but, either way, I'm not going to be learning to crochet any time soon, Dave.

That's what I call self-reinvention, though, and Bowie taught me some great lessons about what it really means to be an

ALL THINGS REMEMBERED

artist. I remember him saying to me once, 'Goldie, did you know Michelangelo said that when you blow the dust off a piece of marble, the sculpture already exists inside?' And that idea has always stayed with me. Oh, wow. God bless you, sir! Yeah, I'm looking up to the sky for you, mate, hearing that little chuckle . . .

F6. More Tales of the Hoffman Process

It sounds melodramatic, I know, but I do think the Hoffman Process saved my life. Apart from anything else, it gave a frame-work within which the times that I'd got really close to leaving the planet – at the end of a really big bag of good-quality cocaine, and some really good-quality vodka, and some really strong Rohypnols – could actually stand me in good stead. Apart from the one I wrote 'Letter of Fate' about, I don't think those were deliberate suicide attempts as such, more just addictive attempts at going somewhere else because of the pain. But if they fucking kill you, then it doesn't really matter what your intentions were, does it? The people left behind still have to pick that one apart. And doing the Hoffman Process gave me my best shot at stopping near misses turning into the real thing.

For anyone who doesn't know about the Hoffman Process – which is probably most people, because it's a bit like *Fight Club* in that you're not really meant to talk about it too much (AA's meant to be like that, too, but that doesn't fucking stop them, does it?) – it's an intense form of therapy which takes place over a short but very concentrated period of time. It's residential, but you only go there for ten days, which doesn't seem like it's going to be enough – I remember I was very sceptical about how little time that seemed beforehand, but once you're there it seems to last for ever. It's kind of like being in the *Big Brother* house in that respect, but without the glass walls that you can see the cameramen through on the other side.

I compare the two experiences like this: I went to Elstree for one, and Seaford – which is between Brighton and Eastbourne

– for the other, met some nutters on both, and obviously you get paid for the first, while the second costs you an arm and a leg, but I know which experience did me more good. The *Big Brother* house is full of people trying to hide who they really are, but the Hoffman Process is for people who want to get to the truth. It's not going to work for everyone, but if you're like I was – trying to get to the bottom of an addiction but frustrated with going to rehab and meeting people who were in there for the third time and still sprinkling crack on their cornflakes – it just might be the one that puts you on the right road.

It's a group thing, a bit cultish, maybe, but not particularly controversial or frowned upon by the medical establishment. You are assigned a therapist who helps you work through a series of different exercises, some of which you do with other people and some on your own. One of the major elements is trying to face up to the demons in your past by writing letters, though I can't divulge too much, because what happens in the Hoffman stays in the Hoffman.

What I can say is that if you think of the issues from earlier life which we all carry round with us as some kind of box in our heads, then the Hoffman doesn't just help you take stuff out of there and have a look at it, it also deals with what fucking branch of IKEA sold you that box and where it was manufactured. So by the end you've got a much better idea of what you're dealing with. Basically, what they're saying is, 'Let's open this fucking box. Pass me that screwdriver . . . you'll need a crowbar for this one. Let's rip it open down the fucking seams. Let's take it back to the flat-pack, and once we've had a look at the instructions, let's go and give the arsehole who designed it a bit of a talking to.'

Before I did the Hoffman, I felt that I had become very destructive – both in terms of my impact on other people and on myself. To be honest, I think I was a complete idiot – one of those people who should be culled with a pair of fucking very big tongs with a big electric spark at the end of them. Addiction makes a complete parody of a person, and I was its willing accomplice. Because, as an addict, you always go back to the same fucking room. I would go in there and sit opposite this fucking thing named pain. It's my Dorian Gray portrait, if you like – my canvas of fucking ill. And it's grotesque, and it's shadowy and it's elusive and it shifts in shape – one moment it's small and in the corner, and the next it's fucking massive and right up in my face. There's nothing else that can be in that room apart from me. Everything else I tried to drag into that room would die a death: relationships, creativity, anything. But what the Hoffman helped me realise, which I found very helpful, is that there is a sense in which my life is already over. Just because my fate is already ordained.

If you think of an ant standing on the kerb outside Ronnie Scott's, it could be that I decide to have another sip of the coffee I'm drinking in the House of St Barnabas round the corner, and that's how our paths cross just at the right moment for me to tread on the ant and end its life – I didn't see it, but I ended it. Or it could be that the extra sip saves him . . . until fucking Wiley walks around the corner going in the opposite direction and does for him.

Either way, there's fuck all the ant can do about it. And in terms of keeping your own significance in perspective as far as the planet as a whole is concerned, there are worse ways to do it than by thinking of yourself as already dead and working your way backwards to now. The planet could be hurtling towards a meteor as we speak. Doesn't matter. All that matters is that the time we're alive for is the blink of an eyelid, so we might as well make the best of it.

Nothing's the answer to everything, obviously. And I'm not exactly a Hoffman Process poster boy. There were certain closure ceremonies you were meant to go to, but I decided not to. I just wanted to try to make it work in my own way and now – more than ten years on – it's something I still refer to constantly in my head. It's certainly what gave me the impetus to get divorced, which is one of the best decisions I've ever made. I'd basically become a womaniser because of my father, and then gone on to marry my mother, which is never the best look, is it?

I do fall off the wagon every once in a while, even now, and I think in terms of dealing with addiction I need a framework which can adapt to that happening – not like AA, where if you so much as have one drink you have to go back to the beginning and start again. I know that works for some people, but not for me, which is partly where my resistance to the whole Eric Clapton thing came from. I think I almost looked at it like Amy Winehouse syndrome – God bless her soul – because sometimes being really, really clean can be very dangerous.

There's a period of time when you're dealing with addiction – well, I say a period of time, but it's probably for ever, because I know I will always be an addict, even though I sometimes manage to shift the energy from one form of addiction to another – when you're like a salmon swimming upstream. You make a bit of progress, and then the current sweeps you back down again. It's a fucking struggle.

It's often when things are going well that you have to watch yourself the most. The last time I fell off the wagon I'd been on a really good run and it just came out of the middle of nowhere. Like in a Punch and Judy show – 'He's behind you! Bam!' Or like when you're playing as a kid and you've wandered away from the garden having a good time and then suddenly you don't know what street you're on or how to get home.

The important thing is the honesty. If you're serious about changing your life, that's the area where there can be absolutely no compromise. So if I've ever gone astray I always have to own up to Mika: 'Babe, I fell off the wagon.' 'Oh, fuck, what did you do?' 'I did two lines of coke and a couple of shots.' Obviously in the old days that would've been a quiet night in, but that's a lot in my world now, because of where it could lead.

The fact that I always feel guilty when it happens is probably a good sign. But it's also important not to carry the guilt too much – just go and do yoga, get back in the lab. I do feel some improvements in myself – in the way I analyse my motivation for doing things, and how I respond to the conclusions I come to. But even when you know exactly what all your set-ups and your sabotages are, that doesn't make them go away. I'll always be the fucking werewolf. The best I can hope for is that I see the full moon coming and say, 'Look, if you love me, chain me up to those fucking iron bars, because when all the howling and the growling's fucking gone and the moon starts to wane, I'll be all right, and I'll thank you for it the next day.'

Addiction is never just about one person's struggle, it's also about what the family have to put up with. My wife has been a big part of this, because she's a very spirited and powerful human being who doesn't have a bad bone in her body. And having someone that you love and want to defend is a big part of any kind of recovery, because it gives you something outside of yourself to focus on and put your trust in. It's never about bettering something for the wrong reason with Mika. Whatever she does, there's never any self-gain in it, it's always about putting someone else before herself.

F7. Yoga

When I was a kid I was often placed alone in rooms, and when that happened I'd turn the TV on, if there was one. Once, when I was in that situation, I saw the famous James Cagney film – I think it's *White Heat* – where at the end he says, 'Made it, Ma – top of the world!' while he's dying in a hail of bullets, and then the whole place blows up. Even though the odds are impossibly stacked against him, he's still going out and getting them in his own mind. It was just that aspect of the film that stuck with me – the aspect of him dying never bothered me, because I was young, when there is no death because no one dies and we live for ever.

In a funny way this was the mentality I took into doing yoga (which is one reason it makes sense for our yoga company to be called 'Yogangsters'). If I want to do yoga, I'm going to do yoga. I'm going to get out there, because I don't care about the hail of bullets. I don't care if you think it's tree-hugging. I'm going to change my life. I'm going to do this. And I'm going to do it to the point where I'm so aggressive with it that I actually break the gravity of those old ideas of what we think it's about, because yoga's culture has to adapt in the same way that the culture of music does.

That's what Yogangsters is all about – 'Guys, your softly, softly fucking approach ain't fucking working.' It's not necessarily that I'm trying to bring aggression to it, more just saying that we should let go of our inhibitions and embrace the effeminate. Do you know what I mean? Hey, guys, note to self: fucking gladiators wore skirts. Vikings, Celtic warriors, fucking have that, you bastards. Wield an axe: fine. You think controlling your fucking aggression is about wearing skinny jeans and a fucking cunt beard in Shoreditch? You think that's going to solve it for me? It's not going to solve it for me. I don't see why grown men can't chase the effeminate by being bare bones about it, by being Neanderthal. Barbecue, smell of burnt meat – why do we still like them? Being in the hot yoga room – what's the difference?

The power of yoga can't be argued with, man. You could be the most horrible fuck in the world – I don't give a bollocks – but you get in that room, and you're going to find yourself somewhere, regardless of how emotional you feel about it, you're going to find yourself. And you will find the good, the bad and the fucking absolutely disgustingly ugly, but you will find yourself.

Michael Kopelman from Stüssy first inspired me to take it up. I was envious of this guy because he always seemed to be in a very calm place. I was like, 'Really? Why the fuck is he always so Zen?' It made me want to punch him in the face, but then when I asked him what his secret was, he said, 'It's yoga, man.' So I took that on board. Even though I resisted it at first, I got there eventually.

Finding yoga was a really important moment in my life, to the point where looking back on it I can see myself in that lonely room as a kid watching that TV, then fast forward and I'm in this room in the self-absorbed age of the selfie, getting to grips with a practice which is generated by looking in the mirror. But this isn't a mirror which shows the best side of you – there are no Instagram filters. It's a mirror where you actually lose all the make-up – not that I wear make-up, but by that I mean all the other camouflage devices of ego and distraction that we use to conceal the disturbing truth – and you begin to really look at yourself.

The first time you look in this mirror and go through the twenty-six postures of Bikram yoga, all of the addictions you've

ALL THINGS REMEMBERED

had in your life just overwhelm you – at least, that's what happened to me. It was as if every drug downer I've ever had – and, obviously, I've had a few – came back to me in one go. It was just, like, '*Argh!*' Totally overwhelming. The first two times this happened, I kind of fell apart and left the room. On the surface it was my ego pulling me out of it – 'Fuck this for a load of bullshit. This ain't right for grown men. What the fuck am I wearing a pair of Speedos for?' Well, to be honest, I didn't start with Speedos, I started with a pair of really fucking baggy shorts, but then you realise that they're retaining 2lbs of water by the end of the session and you think, 'This shit's pulling me down, I'm fucking drowning.' So you kind of adjust to the old budgie-smugglers and realise, 'Fuck me, actually' – this is the ego – 'Actually, you look all right.'

But then something in me said, 'Just go again.' And when I started really sweating – because the room's heated, that's why it's called hot yoga – and crying as I was going through all the back-bending, I started to get it. In the end, back-bending was no problem to me, because back-bending was, 'I want to make it. I want to be on top of the world, Ma – go get 'em.' But forward-bending was really difficult, because it's claustrophobic, like being in an embryo – 'I just know I'm not going to make it, I just know I'm not going to make it,' and the lamenting becomes so loud inside you that you can't hear any other voice over the top of it.

People who don't do it might think yoga is all about physical discipline: it's not about that at all. Well, obviously it is a bit – especially when you've got your head between your legs and you're looking up to see your balls crying with sweat like a baby seal that's about to get clubbed. But it's also about breathing and being free in your movement to hold a position like a fucking sail on a boat. You've got to realise that the outside wind of your energy is maybe pushing you in one way, and the energy which is in the air is maybe pushing you in another direction . . . Are we still? Are we standing on the fucking flagpole's wooden base? Or is that flagpole base vibrating on some other fucking issue that we have?

If you take Bālāsana, the child's pose, for example (which is basically forward-bending with arms extended), I still can't touch both things at the same time, my heels and my arms, partly because it's physically very difficult, but also because of all the emotional baggage that I have. But even if I can move one centimetre closer over a year, that's fine with me. That sense of getting slowly closer to something I want to achieve has been very powerful for me.

Sometimes, after ninety minutes of really hard yoga practice, I think, 'If I could fast forward forty-four and a half minutes from the beginning – erase that – then rewind forty-four and a half minutes back from the end of the class, there's a minute left in the centre of the practice which is the top of the mountain, right?' And I ask myself, as an addict, what I'd pay for that buzz. How much is that worth, man? Because that's some fucking really good gear! You know, that's like the real . . . Peruvian Flake of yin – or the yang, depending on which way you look at it – but it really is some fucking seriously powerful fucking drug.

The thing about it, when you're an addict . . . let's be honest, lads, the first line is everything, the rest is downhill, mate. But yoga is not like that. When you first take cocaine – or any drug for that matter – it's all about the first time. One minute you're thinking, 'What does it do? It's not doing anything.' Two hours later, you're babbling like a fucking supergrass in a fucking Old Bill station . . . But from then on that novelty and that excitement are very hard to recapture. Whereas yoga is not like that. At first you think, 'I feel miserable and I hate myself.' But then you just keep going, and going, and going. I started off once a week, then twice. Then I was going three times a week and then four, and, in the end, it became an obsession, like six times a fucking week – hang on: timeout! Your schedule doesn't allow it and then you back off a little bit, and you realise that, because you've put the work in, you know, it's OK. So now I can do three practices a week and I'm fucking great. I meet my quota.

The point about yoga is how it makes you feel: I feel like a child again, I feel like I can breathe, you know? I used to go to the gym all the time and, believe me, there's some boys that are pushing a lot of weight and it's great, it's fantastic. Every man will admit – well, maybe won't admit – but you're sitting there, and it's like a fucking theatre show: you're waiting to see if another guy notices how well you're doing at the peak of your fucking exercising. Of course, some guys are more disciplined than that. They're more like the guy that does fucking martial arts but he won't even start a pub fight, because he's not into it – he's about defence, not attack. That's not me, though. I'm all about giving it the fucking big 'un and chucking it around like nobody's business.

So, yeah, you can pump up and everything else, but after a while it starts to dawn on you that it's all about holding your breath. Let's get these weights – *aahhhh . . . grunt . . . ooargh* – I wasn't sure how to fucking notate that, by the way, but I've had a really good crack at putting it in writing. When you're lifting weights, all the force has to be held inside – you're holding your breath. But yoga's the opposite: it's not holding your breath, it's about . . . breathing. For the first couple of years I was still hold-ing my breath; the third year, kind of learning not to hold my breath; and then after four or five years it gets really interesting . . . And now I'm at seven.

Who would have thought that I'd be the person trying to tell everyone how important yoga is? I certainly wouldn't have. I was never into it, but then all of a sudden I was, and I started thinking, 'Who is this fucking guy, this cocky prick, this geezer who will just jump down your throat with some arrogant bollocks?' Yeah, that's me. Do you know what I mean? 'What an obnoxious twat!'

One reason why I think it's a really good idea for yoga to be taught in schools and prisons is not just for the physical well-being it gives you, but also for the mental conditioning. I should say at this point that I have no desire to become a yoga teacher. My partner in my yoga business – my adopted little sister, Kelly – is a qualified teacher, and Bikram Choudhury (who Bikram yoga is named after) once asked me himself: 'Goldie, come to teacher training, come to me' – I can do a very good Bikram impression, but if you don't know him you're going to have to take this on trust – 'I want you to do this, Goldie, fantastic, come and do teacher training with us.'

The reason I don't want to do that is because I know how my ego works – I'll start thinking I'm a guru and just become a dick. Then I'll become complacent and stop training. I've actually seen quite a lot of yogis get caught up in the ego of how great it all is, and I know how susceptible I'd be to that. Even today while I'm thinking about this – and where am I? I'm in London in a hotel – I can feel my ego leading me down the wrong path. I'm going to Ireland later, and I was just thinking, 'Yeah, I'm off to Dublin, I'll put on my Yeezys . . .' Duh! It's raining, you idiot – wear boots!

Finding a good yoga teacher is like finding a really good lover. You find new ways of inventing shit with them. The more you throw at them, and the more disgruntled you become with your own practice, the more they'll improve it. I'm in no sense a yogi; I'm a student of yoga. I've learned from people like Paul

Dobson, Cindy Hague (now married to another exceptional yogi, Michael) and Michele, who runs Fierce Grace, in the same way I learned from the great graffiti writers or Marc and Dego, and it's important for me to have that relationship. I've got to stay on the mat – that's what it's all about. That's why the best place for me to be as far as yoga is concerned is in the fucking trenches with the soldiers, rallying the troops. It's what Jimmy Cagney would've wanted.

SIDE G

G1. From Russia with . . . Multiple Fractures of the Left Hand

I'm left-handed. I always lean that way, whatever I'm doing. I do graffiti with my left hand. I lead with my left hand if I'm fighting – a Walsall southpaw, that's me. As a result I've broken it nine times now. Mostly in fights. It's more of a club than a hand these days. It's got no feeling in it – hard to believe there's even any circulation, if medical science can encompass that.

The last time I had to use it to drill someone with was about five years ago, in a first-class airport lounge in Russia, when I had to iron out a rugby player. I'm not proud of myself – it's the kind of thing I'm trying to stop happening and, to be fair, I've not done it since – but I can't very well call this book *All Things Remembered* and not put something like this in, can I?

I was wearing the Bronx t-shirt that gets me into a lot of trouble. Tats Cru: the Bronx. There was a fucking Harlequins fan, or some shit – a big feller, either way – in a fucking first-class British Airways lounge in Russia. I'd finished one gig and I was on my way to the next, but I suppose the story really starts with me losing my silver feather – or, rather, having it stolen by Russian airport security – which was really annoying.

The silver feather was a Goro – i.e. it was made by a really fucking famous Japanese jewellery designer who is no longer with us. One in, one out of the shop at Harrods – that's how this shit goes. It had been introduced to me by the Stüssy crew: Michael Kopelman; Alex Baby definitely had one; Miles, Lord Barnsley and Fraser Cooke probably did too.

'What the fuck is that?' It's kind of B-boy supreme – you have to know what it is. Always wanted one, got the final blessing to go get one, got it. Then I'm in airport security, and the woman asks me for my ticket. The flight's in forty minutes. I take the chain off, put it in the tray, it goes through the machine. Now I step through, put the hands up. All of a sudden, I see the tray going back into security, don't think anything of it, but the girl on the side I just came from has lifted it and fucked off – taken it, gone. The tray comes back and I look in it – 'Where's my fucking chain?' They're all pretending to look. 'Oh, in the machine, it might have dropped.' They know I've got to get the flight, suddenly no one speaks English any more. Bam: stolen.

Losing something on a beach is different, man: somebody's going to find something and it's going to be very beautiful and they gain something. But this is someone – and someone in a position of trust – specifically, malevolently stealing a piece from you. And getting away with it. So that really made me very, very angry.

I went to the next gig, and I was still fucking fuming, so I got on the old fucking Russian Standard vodka. Over the years, I've been known to be quite infamous for what happens when I'm on that stuff, and I was in the back room of this place where the gig had happened when two kids came in – young drum 'n' bass guys. They sat down by the door and one of them said something, I don't know what it was – I just destroyed the door, pounded and pounded the fucking door till it was off its hinges. It was like papier fucking mâché.

The next day, I'd kind of calmed the fuck down and I'd gone back to the airport, but I was still waiting for some cunt to light the touchpaper, you know? It's not so much the fact that some-one's stolen from me that's really got me fucking angry, it's the way she did it. I have respect for cat burglars: they go in, no locks are broken, you don't even know it's missing, it's gone.

Bam. Bank fraud: fucking hell, wow! But the way she used the fact that I had to get the flight against me makes this feel more like the dirty fucking burglar that shits and pisses on your carpet and fucking leaves a stain and hasn't got a clue. They're the ones I fucking despise. I can't stand those cunts. You're not the Pink Panther, baby. Take the whole fucking car instead of just trying to take the stereo, you knob-head. That's why removable fascias were invented, for cunts like you.

So, you know, anyway, I'm in the lounge, I've lost the feather. I've already spoken to Michael, and he's said, 'I'll get you another one, G,' which he actually does and I'm very thankful for it, even though it is a little bit smaller. For the moment, though, it's gone. The security woman's thieved it. In Russia. I'm in the fucking lounge, I'm wearing the Bronx t-shirt and I get up to go and get some coffee, when this rugby-shirt guy goes, 'Oh, "the Bronx", yeah? . . . Ain't Leeds, is it?'

'What?'

'It's not Leeds, is it?'

'What do you mean, "It's not Leeds"? You cunt. Leeds is full of fucking students.'

'What did you call me?'

I go, 'Mate, listen, not now . . .' But he's not going to leave it, so then I just take one step towards him and say, 'Cunt. C-U-N-T. Cunt.' And the geezer, I think he's a bit shocked, really, because he's a big feller. But half a second later I see him rock back on his heels, so he's changing his body position, and as he changes his body position I feel the wind of the glance as he takes a swing at me and I duck it. At that point I just pull his hoodie up over his shoulders and start pounding the fuck out of him.

Larry Calyx and Teebee, two drum 'n' bass guys who like to give it the big 'un sometimes, are sitting there in the lounge like baby lambs. I guess they're thinking, '*Argh!* We just want to go home.' I mean, God bless Larry, but he has got a fucking head like a news presenter, and Teebee goes bright red sometimes, but they're still my guys. At least they were until they sat there like fucking idiots when it was all kicking off instead of backing me up. Teebee talks a good game when it comes to kung fu, but he Jet Li'd out of that movie pretty sharpish at the first sign of trouble.

It's OK, it's all right. I don't mind that you didn't help me later on when all the shit went off with the people on the desk and you left me at the gate and I had to wait five hours for the next flight. But I did hear afterwards that Teebee apparently said to someone, 'Oh, Goldie's a right nightmare – you can't take him anywhere.' Now I will be the first to admit that at some times in my life there's been truth in that, but in this case, no. Get it right. In this case, Goldie just stood his fucking ground.

This is in Russia, in a first-class lounge. And I'm minding my own business, and the guy's like, 'Ah, the Bronx, it ain't Leeds, is it?' What else am I gonna do? It's not like it's the forties any fucking more in Leeds, is it? It's all gentrified and full of students now. I can't let him have it. So I do let him have it. Unfortunately, ironing him out comes at a cost. Straight away my hand's swelled up like a fucking football – I've taken two out of the joint, snapped it a couple of times. The Harlequins guy is not looking too clever either – there's claret everywhere, but the funny thing is, he's apologising. Sincerely as well – 'Oh, I'm really sorry, I shouldn't have.' So the good manners the rugby people are meant to have come through eventually, once he's covered in blood! I can't believe it – he's cunting apologising!

At that point, the Russian police turn up – in the big high hats. And of course the guy speaks perfect Russian. Here we go. Here we fucking go. So I'm waving my gold card around telling them, 'Go and look at your fucking camera and you can clearly

see that he's taken a swing at me. And he's missed. Bad luck!'
That's what me and my guys always say – 'Bad luck!' I've even
had t-shirts printed that say it. Oh, he's going to school – bad
luck! Looks like a cunt – bad luck! It comes up a lot playing *Call
of Duty*: tried to shoot me from behind the hedge – bad luck! In
this instance, of course, it's not *Call of Duty*, it's real life, but the
law of bad luck still applies. Maybe even more so. Tried to iron
me out but got more than you bargained for – bad luck!

So, anyway, they can't arrest me. Nothing bad happens. They
send us home on separate flights and I have to get the later one
– that's the only bad consequence, apart from me having to go to
Watford General Hospital at two in the morning. Once I've got
the X-ray, they say, 'Fuck me, you've broken your fucking hand.'
No shit, Sherlock. It costs me six and a half bags to put the hand
right (bag of sand = grand). Harley Street, let's not fuck this up:
bars, wires, bam, bam, you know? It's cost me.

I guess one of the morals of this story is, even if you're right,
it can still be fucking wrong. Obviously, because that shit's still
deep in me, part of me is thinking, 'This is a great bit of pub
talk,' and whatever else. The feller was big, so I've done really
well to iron him out – lovely, fantastic, still got it, keeping it
sharp, pat on the back, etc. But on the other hand – which in
this case is broken – you've got nothing if you can't rise above
it. This has cost me six and a half bags! You could put a fucking
kid through school with that. And he's probably sitting there in
the pub in Leeds going, 'Oh, mate, Goldie's a nightmare, and I'm
never going to the fucking Bronx.'

But I'm not just some dick wearing a t-shirt from the Bronx,
I've got a connection with the place. Tats Cru are my crew. So
you're trying to think you're hard? The Bronx ain't rough, mate.
I could've had a t-shirt that said, 'The Gorbals' – in Glasgow,
right? Leave it out! You know it's an area. You're saying Leeds is

a general fucking hole, but you're probably not from a really dirty hard part – because there are some hard parts of Leeds. You're a fucking rugby fan in a branded shirt who speaks Russian, with loads of money and a Russian bird. You ain't from Leeds really, son. Not in a Harlequins shirt. That's my point. You should know better, you cunt. And you are a cunt, because I called you one. Now fuck off.

So anyway, it's done. But I suppose the other moral of the story from my point of view, which is quite an interesting one, is that it's not ever really quite done. Because of the time of my life I was at – this was years after I'd done the Hoffman – I sort of thought my getting-in-fights-in-first-class-airport-lounges days were behind me. But I get my silver feather nicked and there I am back to my old ways – filling up with the old Royal Standard and steaming in, but I think that's what happens with the Hoffman. You still wriggle around like a snake in the box for a while afterwards; you wrap around the sides of it a little bit. Imagine being locked in a coffin: you're fucking tapping on the lid from the inside. Oh, I've got to breathe here and work a way out of this . . . now the saw's coming through. At last . . .

G2. *The Journey Man* II – the Drums: Texturing the Abyss

Three years ago, I spent two days doing the most amazing drum sessions at Battery Studios in Willesden, redoing every classic drum-break and breaking down every new idea to a motif we could slow down to a pattern that could be explained to a drummer who could then play it. Part of the excitement of this was, 'OK, so let's go into my favourite records of all time. Now I can time-travel through technology and take the car fucking sideways.' But it wasn't just about looking at the beats of Can or Herbie Hancock or any other artist I really respect and thinking, 'How can I reproduce this and at the same time take it somewhere else?' It was also about establishing a way of working which was a creative process in its own right.

The ninety-seven takes we came out with generally involved three different players: two drummers and one percussionist. John Blease was usually set up in the main studio, with Adam Betts in a closed room and Hugh Wilkinson somewhere else doing percussion over the top. We miked it all up, and we spent, say, half an hour on each break – all hammering away at the same motif, whether together or individually. When we had all those breaks done, I gave one copy to James Davidson of Ulterior Motive, who I knew was going to engineer the album with me, and I took the other one to Thailand, where I sat on it for a year. The reason I did that was to gain a bit of distance and also show my respect, because when you go back to them, you know the first rhythmic idea you hear is going to be super-important; in fact, it's probably going to be the one.

This probably sounds crazy, but from the beginning of my career I've always bounced sounds onto DAT – to create more space. At first we'd record sounds on a sixteen-track desk, so we'd have maybe three breaks running on a single channel, then we'd mix them and bounce them back to DAT so they're kind of contained, like an analogue sound in a digital bubble. Then we'd take those three breaks that are now on DAT and sample them back to ourselves on a single channel. I'm always interested in the residue that's left behind when two sounds are banging up against each other, but then you mute the original two and record the ghost. What we're doing all the time is creating these layers. It's like texturing the abyss.

And if you're going into the abyss, you couldn't have a better guide than Adam Betts. In the nineties, some of the drummers who tried to manually reproduce the complexity of the beats we were working with really struggled. It was something to do with the way that we edited them together, that kind of B-boyism in the breaks, if you will. It's a bit like the way James Brown is all about being on the one, and if you go too far away from that or become too complex, it just loses the vibe and the soul of the whole thing. But the way that Adam has studied drumming over the years – maybe it's because he originally came from a punk band – seems to have given him a different entry point where he can just walk through the virtual hallways of drum 'n' bass rhythm like he owns the place. He's a new evolutionary form of drummer, in the same way that Ronaldo's like a higher species of footballer: the ball, like the drum-skin, might not have changed much, but the way he's adapted to its movement it's like he's speaking a new language.

When I came back to those drums a year later, they already sounded fucking unbelievable. And that was even before James had gone to work on all of them. The process he put them through was a kind of dehumanising filter ('taking the pop bottle out of it' they used to call it, because of the popping sound which is the telltale sign of human involvement) – basically doing digital damage to them so they come out as a really fierce hybrid, still themselves but now kind of on steroids, really beautiful and round and accentuated.

The processing of breaks has come on in leaps and bounds. It's not about finding the loudest fucking snare and side-chain – it's more about the overall fucking sound of it. So when James came out to Thailand at the beginning of April 2016, we sat in that studio and we listened to those breaks, going through the ones James had already processed and the ones he hadn't. It was a little bit like a Specsavers commercial: better with, or better without? It was always better with – they were essentially the same, but he would take them up to a whole other level of solidity and detail.

Then we went through all the takes we'd chosen and whittled them down to maybe the twenty or twenty-five best. That was really exciting because I couldn't wait to revisit them. The brushwork that Betts had done in particular I thought was amazing – people hadn't really pushed working with brushes in the drum 'n' bass fold before, as it's seen more as something from the jazz world, but it was something I wanted to do, and I think it was a really successful experiment. Having these rhythmic shapes which John, Adam and Hugh had made with me, I knew almost straight away which song was going to be which. I couldn't wait to sprinkle my own history onto them – the thirty-five years of what I'd liked, whether it was 'Long Dark Tunnel', or Chromatone's remix, a bit of Metheny here, a bit of Beck there.

That's the illusionist stuff, where you go, 'Here's my magic show, but you can't see the wires or the trap door. Both my hands are clearly visible and the music is coming out of two fucking speakers.' Before the sound, you hear the colour of the beats, and hopefully that synaesthesia kind of washes over and through the Attention Deficit Disorder and all the other fucking ailments the syntheticness of our environment and all of the gadgets and the information and the different wavelengths clogging up the air seem to have made so much worse for everyone. All the other pigments might have bled away into pastel shades, but these drum-breaks don't run. James made sure of that – he is meticulous.

I was a very angry young man when *Timeless* came out. Even though I was thirty, that album felt like my adolescence. Basically, it's me going, 'Yeah, fucking *Timeless*, fuck you all, fuck the fucking system.' And the reason I was doing that is because I was still carrying all of this fucking daddy shit, all of these mummy issues. Puberty should've been long behind me at that point, but I was still carrying all of this stuff: it's like a coming of age thing, even today.

I'd been in Wolverhampton, in the ghetto. After spending pretty much my entire life in the care system, when I was eighteen I was free and I was off to find my mother. The lamenting for the loss of her had been constant throughout my life. And then I found her, and I found this really fucked-up, broken family that was my own bloodline. So I kind of accepted that.

But then, of course, came the persecution of my mother. My mum's life was to blame for everything: I had 'victimitis', as many young people do. The truth was I was fucking angry at my old man for coming here and blazing my mum and going to America and running away. And I was angry at my mum for taking that shit. But at the same time I'm sitting there in the fucking 'hood thinking, 'OK, I know I'm British. I don't know what colour I am, but I do know I'm fucking proud to be a kid of black origin – so I'm a fucking mulatto. What's it to you?'

I was a very, very angry guy, because of my abandonment issues, and I was also a fucking kung fu expert. So I'd just walk straight into the fucking room and fight everyone. Even if they're not fighting you, then fight them anyway for the sake of

it, because everyone's going down. I just didn't give a fuck. And thanks to my chronic case of victimitis, literally nothing could ever be my fault.

My dad wouldn't have got far with that attitude. He came here on the sixties wave from the Caribbean islands that helped build this country. He fucking grafted. He worked at Ford's in Dagenham, and then in Leeds. He met my mum in a pub, and she was a pub singer. And they fell in love – God bless them. And he was up and down the M1, he was running around, and my mum would wait for him endlessly, and she suffered the emotional pain that I couldn't empathise with until it was almost too late.

I think it's only when you get older that you realise, 'I used to really hate olives, but I really love them now.' And that empathy which I eventually found for my mother went into that difficult second album, where, of course, I could have played the record-company game, but I wanted to make 'Mother' instead. It was very important to me because of the empathy that I'd found for her. She came from the Gorbals in Scotland, her father was an alcoholic, his father was an alcoholic, she became a dancer, she fell in love with two black men at the same time who both promised her the world. And I was a product of that.

I think what the Hoffman Process helped me realise was that a lot of us who are damaged goods in one way or another tend to gravitate towards feeling sorry for ourselves. That's what I mean by victimitis. My drug addiction was very bound up with that. And it's the same with all the replacement addictions people find for themselves – whether that be religion, yoga, water-skiing, backgammon. It's amazing the things people will manage to get addicted to. Obviously sex is one of the more logical ones. I was addicted to pussy at one stage in my life – tell me what young man ain't. But we just have to look inside ourselves to find the love and understanding that will stop us being so cruel to ourselves and to others.

The nineties were very hedonistic for me – I went down this complete *Alice in Wonderland* rabbit hole; I didn't quite come back out, in some respects. At first drug use is really enjoyable, but then when the party finishes and the drugs end and you're looking around for your next dealer, that's when the victimitis tends to kick in – there's this inherent tendency to buy into all the fucking doom and gloom, and just to feel like you've been fucking hard done by. I definitely had a bit of that when I went to Eric Clapton's rehab. His intention was to heal, but I couldn't deal. The suspicion that somewhere along the way I seem to have paid for one of the wheel nuts on his fucking Ferrari Enzo probably didn't help. But sometimes when you're feeling slightly robbed in that kind of situation, you have to ask yourself who you're really robbing by letting that feeling take over. However much the victimitis card might look like a winner, you'll always lose by playing it.

I saw a bit of the same kind of anger and defensiveness in my daughter, Chance, for a while, but I think she's getting over it now – which is good, because she's definitely got a genetic inheritance to process in that area. The reason I'm so good at diagnosing victimitis in others is obviously because I had such a terrible case of it myself. But eventually – with a lot of help from the Hoffman Process, and yoga, and Mika, and Chance – I stopped accompanying myself on an invisible fucking violin and just manned up and got on with it. The funny thing about manning up is, it also means you have to find the inner child and go, 'Oh, this child created Goldie as a form of protection, but then the Goldie that was created became a little bit like a Pandora's box that opened up, and so much bad shit came out that the child got crushed by a tsunami of fucking sewage.'

In that situation, you just have to let time do its thing, until you finally see a glimmer of hope. For me that glimpse came when I saw myself in the mirror striving to do yoga and thought, 'Fuck, there is somebody in there that I used to love – that kid who took me into music in the first place, the kid who got me to New York.' That was the beginning of my rehabilitation as a human being – I wanted to live.

G4. The Time Machine

Where am I? I'm in my house in Thailand, in early 2017, downstairs in an atrium, looking at the giant stump of a tree that fell down into the forest six months ago, and the stump is square in the window, and it looks like the tree goes all the way up, but it doesn't. It's a beautiful window, though, and there's a piano standing in front of it. And I'm on the borderline of joyful and tearful, because this is one of those moments when the present becomes a bit like a hummingbird for me, because it's moving so fast that you can actually find a bit of stillness in it. At that point, remembering becomes less of a trauma – which is good, because when you've got a lot of bad memories like I have, you tend to block everything out, but that way you lose the ability to remember the good things as well.

So anyway, we've been having some freak weather in Asia. It's like a monsoon again in January, which is almost unheard of. I guess it's like that all around the world these days, because Mother Nature's very angry. And no wonder, 'cos she keeps telling us, 'Don't build shit on the cracks in my china,' but we don't listen, then when the whole thing falls apart she always gets the blame.

Here I am, watching all of the water drip down this fucking tree, and thinking about the years and years it's taken this tree to grow. It's over a hundred years old, and the water's running down it like the veins standing out on my arm during yoga. It's beautiful to watch.

I'm also thinking to myself about how strong this tree used to be – she was 120 feet tall, but last year she became cancerous around the base and her inside got hollowed out at the bottom, and then she became saturated and fell into the forest. I had the trunk gracefully cut up – made sure they did it neatly – and had all of her pieces put back into the forest. But a good 12–14 foot of her remains in the base of the house and goes to the first-floor balcony, and levels off there. Inside it's hollow, because of the cancer of the tree – it is inevitable to all of us that in this physical realm we will all wither and die.

What I did with the hollowed-out tree was I filled it full of beautiful dirt, beautiful earth. And I'm going to put loads of plants inside, and they'll all grow out of the tree, and new life will come, new lizards will find homes, and everything else. I suppose the point I'm trying to make is, in the billions of years of the universe's existence, all we really are is one spark of energy in a massive fucking web of intrigue.

There was an aspect of the Hoffman Process which also helped with that realisation. You had to do this fire ceremony, and there was a particular piece of wood in the flames that had all but burnt away. As I walked around the fire at the end of the ceremony, the charred remnant seemed to move towards me. Then as I walked back the other way, it seemed to move towards me again. Just as I was freaking out, thinking, 'Fuck, what's going on here?' the rest of it just collapsed and all these cinders flew into the sky. As they dissipated you couldn't tell if they were cinders or stars, and the odd crackle touched your skin with that sharp needle-prick of dust and carbon.

It made me feel like an animal. Your skin's already been ripped off your body by the whole process of going through the Hoffman, and now this happens! The next morning, and I'm not going to give too much away about this, you have to go back out into nature to find something. So you run out into the fields, and I went to the fire, and I found the tiny bit of wood that was left and I started scratching away at it with this little penknife that my friend had given me before I went into the Hoffman. I was scraping away all the charred stuff and paring away the layers, and in the end there were just these three knots left in the wood – it looked like the head of a narwhal. I soaked it in some Arabian oil and I remember just rubbing it in my hands and feeling it and smelling it – just this very natural, primal scent that it had.

Years later, in 2013, I did an art show at the Mead Carney gallery in Mayfair called *Lost Tribes*, which had a very strong African and Native American influence. This was when I was still living in Hertfordshire, but I collected timber for it from nearby woodland – sniffing around for wobbly tree roots like some mad urban hog looking for truffles. I'd unearth them and pull them out, then bring them home on the back of my mate Richie the gardener's flat-bed truck. All the time I was thinking about how far I'd come since that incident with the wood in the fire at the Hoffman, and kind of lamenting the whole process at the same time.

What started off as a show of eighteen pieces ended up being twenty-seven. I went hell for leather on those paintings, but I also got really into the whole process of sandblasting. When you see people doing refurbs on old buildings in London, and they've got these big cloth covers all over them, what's usually going on inside is the old stone is being sandblasted to clean it up and remove all the layers of grime. My premise was to do the same thing but working on wood, so I'd get the helmet and the big gloves on and there I was, blasting away. It was powerful shit, man, like that old film *The Time Machine*, just watching the layers of years and years of growth coming off the tree root. It's a beautiful thing to watch – as powerful as seeing the gold melt in the crucible. You're physically time-travelling through this piece of wood, and by the end of that process I had eight or nine of these big, sandblasted roots that just looked absolutely beautiful. Especially once I'd kind of planted them in the middle of the gallery.

Most of the roots I found tended to be oak, but there was one particular piece that was birch, and when I pulled it out of the ground – this was shortly before the whole move to Thailand happened in terms of the land finally becoming available, and in retrospect it felt like a massive sign – it just looked amazing, like the skull of an antelope or a gazelle. So I took it and sandblasted enough of it away so what was left looked even better, and I called it *Picasso's Nature* because it was so beautiful. Somebody offered me fifteen grand for it when it was on display at the Mead Carney, but me being really fucking self-indulgent and stupid, I respectfully refused the offer on the following grounds: 'Of all the work, this is the one thing I want to keep – buy a fucking painting, you twat.'

Another reason that water-skiing accident on *The Games* was beautiful was because it saved me from something a lot worse happening. I was driving Ferraris a little too fast at the time. Me and my co-pilot Moose, who is still one of the tightest fellers for me. Moose, man – Derek, Big Moose, MC Moose's brother – he's got good Jamaican DNA. His wife Jessica was my PA for many years and I'm godfather to his kids – they live over in Ruislip now. He's proper Stonebridge, though – physically, he's solid like iron, done good, knows the value of a fireplace. I like that, when man gets seasoned, and he's from the 'hood, but he can look at a fireplace and tell you what it's worth.

I've known Moose for years – he used to run promotions and do Roller Express. I remember the veteran reggae DJ David Rodigan saying to me, 'When you get a "forward" from the back of the room, that's when it really counts' – because that means the older men are in the back and they're enjoying it. That's Moose – from the back of the room, he knows. No two tune, no two riddim he can't pick apart, because he's been around. Our little firm that used to run about at Twice as Nice on Sunday nights in UK garage days was me, Moose, Rhino from *Gladiators* and a guy called Ilya, who's a jeweller and actually has a good voice and can shuffle good foot as a bonus.

Anyway, the point I'm trying to get to is that me and Moose moved hard on the road. We beat someone up outside Capital Radio once for throwing a peanut at the Ferrari. That's how out of control we were. A few years later, in the months before the Beautiful Accident, we'd get in the Ferrari and go lashing up to Leeds in an hour and fifty minutes or something ridiculous – an hour and forty-two minutes from Hertfordshire, I think that was the record. One hundred and seventy-five miles per hour is probably not a sensible speed unless you're on a racetrack. I'd take that car to the limit – no point in having the stereo on because you couldn't hear yourself speak. But then a couple of times – because that was when my horrible mess of a divorce was happening – I'd wake up on the driveway with an empty bottle of vodka in the car, thinking, 'You fucking git, you're gonna kill yourself – and, worse than that, you're gonna kill someone else.'

This was right after I'd done the Hoffman, but obviously the new sobriety was taking a while to bed in. I hadn't fully worked it out yet – hadn't fully realised that I'd married someone who was never going to love me the way I wanted to be loved. Effectively I'd married my fucking mother. It was wrong, but it was a phase of life that I needed to go through. The same as the divorce was. But in a way the half a million it was costing me and the water-skiing accident were a price worth paying. Because those were the reasons I got rid of all the motors. And if I hadn't got rid of the motors – sold them all before I fucked off to Thailand – I'd have been wrapped around a tree, dead.

My dad's ninety-two – still strong, his dad lived to about 102. We have very strong genes in the Price family, but that tradition could have been cut short by me being a complete twat: 'G came up, did his thing, blah-blah-blah, big money tings, Ferraris, Bentleys . . .' I look back on that now and think, 'What a fucking mug!' It's that whole 'Another nigger next year' thing, isn't it? We're not used to that kind of money which comes as you're coming up, when all of a sudden you're the fucking man and you're going to live for ever. Next thing you know you're sitting there with all your money out on the driveway, thinking, 'What the actual fuck?' A Ferrari, a Bentley, a Porsche, and it's three in the afternoon, you're buzzing off your nut and you don't want to go outside and drive them. What a mug. On a good day, yeah, I get it. But when I think about it, it was the same shit. Because I did the same regressive shit that we all do. So it all had to go.

I had to get rid of them, even the Cosi, which had been in storage for years. The Cosi was the first record-deal car I ever bought – a Mercedes Cosworth sixteen-valve dog-leg (which means the first gear's down and on the left). Black, beautiful, immaculate – I was the first person in London that was bussin' chrome rims. Parked it outside Raw Club, sitting there with its fucking chrome rims – everyone's going, 'Man, G's come down in a Mercedes, man.' It's the same Mercedes Derrick May jumped in the back of outside Black Market Records – I had a ridiculous system in that car, it was louder than fucking Black Market at the time. Fucking mental. Anyway, happy memories, and most importantly I'm still around to enjoy them. At least at the time of fucking writing I am, anyway. Thanks, Channel 4 and the law-yers: you – and the Beautiful Accident – fixed it for me to pay off that woman, get rid of everything and start a new life. Now that's what I call public service broadcasting . . .

I've reached that time of my life where you have friends that are dying. Well, to be honest, it's always been that time of my life. But now we're all a bit older it is interesting to sit with those friends and talk to them honestly and not pity them as they get near the end. Whitey – whose real name was Ian Whitehouse – was a big influence on my life back in the Wolverhampton days, in the eighties. He gave me my first real job at his screenprinting workshop, and really boosted my confidence by having faith in my designs. In return I gave him his nickname to differentiate him from the guy who introduced us, whose name was Ian White.

Ian White owned a factory but was also working the markets in Wolverhampton, and he was telling me where he got his stuff printed, and I wanted to get someone to do some for me, because I'd signed up for one of those Prince's Trust things that gave you some funding to do some t-shirts. Looking back, that was kind of a natural stepping stone between the graffiti and the gold teeth – moving through the gears between two and three dimensions – but I didn't know that at the time. I was just airbrushing Wildstyle t-shirts and needed to find a printer, and me and the first Ian had this strange arrangement of me renting a place off him that didn't really work out, but it was through him that I found Whitey, and then Whitey gave me a job and we became really close friends.

Whitey eventually died of the toxic inhalation he'd experienced in the course of his old job, which involved taking asbestos off roofs. But when I first got to know him he was running his own screenprinting place in Wolverhampton. He had a dental chair that I used to sit in and watch them all printing – it was a six-carousel set-up, and Whitey used to supply t-shirts to be sold in Camden Market, right outside the Oxford Arms. The guy was still there last time I looked, but he's probably gone now. The drop-off was in New North Road in Islington, so we'd have to drive all the t-shirts down there from Wolverhampton. They were the classic English t-shirts of the time, which was the late eighties: Joy Division, the flag, 'I like the pope, the pope smokes dope', the tie-dye stuff and the eyes that came in with acid house.

By this time I was going to the Wag Club when I was down in London, and from there it was Paul Oakenfold's club, Spectrum, at Heaven on a Monday. The second time I went to America – to meet up with my dad in Miami – Whitey took me to the airport in his fucking Citroën 2CV – the one that's flat at the back, looks a bit like a VW Beetle. I know it was 1988, because it was when 'Fast Car' by Tracy Chapman had just come out. Whitey put it on as he drove me to the airport. We were two grown men but we cried like babies in that airport. It wasn't the end of our friendship, though, because we did loads together after I came back too: among other things, printing Soul II Soul t-shirts – like the big head with the brown and sepia letters, the poetry. That was us. And I did t-shirts for the Brain club when that came along, and me and Whitey worked together on my own merchandise after things started to blow up for me too.

Whitey was sixteen years older than me, but he was one of those older guys – Gus Coral would be the main one, but there have been others – who have given me a bit of fatherly guidance along the way, the kind I never got from people I was actually related to. So I was really gutted when he died.

Not long after Whitey's death I was in Thailand, in Phuket town, when something really strange and beautiful happened. I was walking around an old gift shop full of Godzillas, old pieces of Chopper bikes and loads of fucking tiny Matchbox cars. For some reason I didn't understand I started going through them – looking and looking – until finally I saw it. One light, champagne-coloured Citroën 2CV, just like the one Whitey used to drive. What were the chances of finding that there?

I bought it, took it home and put it in the prayer house in Thailand. It's on the shelf by the piano. Call this faith, call it whatever you like – I'm still looking into it, but it's enough to satisfy my soul for the moment. And either way, Whitey was a fucking great guy, and I was lucky to have been able to count him as a friend.

My old tour manager, Cliff Whyte, was another close friend who passed away – this time, in late 2016, from pancreatic cancer; the fucking Big C. Sometimes I'll drive through Kamala high street, near where I live now in Thailand, and there's a Tesco's type of supermarket chain called The Big C. If you've come from Europe, you're like, 'What the fuck?'

Cliff was a legend in the hip-hop game. Public Enemy, De La Soul, he tour-managed them all. He'd been there and he'd done that. He was Birmingham born and bred, from a big family, and unfortunately he'd lost his mother and his brother in the same way that he finally went, so it was definitely one of these things where there's this trail of destruction through the whole bloodline, and it was just really sad. He didn't feel well on a tour, he felt a bit sick, he kept feeling lethargic; he went back home, he went to the hospital, and that was it. They gave him six months, and then, fuck, it was like three weeks. What a tragedy – only fifty-six, and he left behind Kylie and three kids.

All manner of crazy shit went on when we were on tour with Jane's Addiction and Perry Farrell. You know, blow-up dolls on the tour bus, going to Vegas and spending fifteen, twenty grand in a fucking casino. Rock 'n' roll shit. I think the single thing I remember most was wanting to get into fights and Cliff just putting his hand on your fucking chest and your head, and you're fucking swinging and whatever else, and then he just picks you up and puts you under his arm. God bless him, he was my tour manager for two, three tours, and the memories that we had together are just so fucking beautiful, and horrendous, and funny. For some reason when he died I immediately thought of the time when he carried me offstage in Atlanta, and I was going, 'Welcome to Atlantic City,' which is not a good look when you're in Atlanta.

Soon after Cliff's death, I spoke to Kylie – who was obviously in bits – and asked her, 'Have you got anything, any pictures of him, so I can put them in the prayer house?' Because in Thailand we have these prayer houses, and when people die we put things up, we burn a candle and incense. It's a really nice tradition. And so Kylie says, 'I've got these wonderful pictures of you and him and Ice-T,' and it opened up this whole line of thought.

Cliff was the one who introduced me to Ice when he was Body Count's tour manager. He was Ice-T's main man and he took me to meet him on the set of *CSI*. And Public Enemy – oh my God! I remember how much they meant to me when I came back from New York and I used to be running around in a leather jacket and a fucking Troop tracksuit. Standing in the Birmingham Hummingbird, watching Public Enemy – that was the business. I went there in a fucking Toyota Corolla – you know, tripped out, chrome rims, all this bullshit. I rolled up thinking I was the shit, and when you look back, well . . . it looked American at the time. I guess it's just like your fucking school classroom: it looks really good when you're in it as a kid, then you go back years later as an adult and you see that it was tiny.

How I first met Cliff was that he was part of Russell Simmons's company Rush Management, and he came to London with

Trenton, my old manager. He'd done all the tours, but Fuji Rock Festival: oh, man! We were in this really traditional Japanese hotel, and we'd been at it for a few days – fucking madness, running around. And I think Primal Scream were out there, Bobby and Mani – I fucking love them. We're all getting hammered and I'm onstage going, 'Moshi moshi, Tokyo, fucking Fuji Rock!' Then when we're coming back, Bobby Gillespie's got this fucking chrome German helmet on, and he's going, 'Goldie, man, I mean, me, you, UB40, Slade, smashing it, in't we,' and I'm like, 'Fucking hell.' Slade came from Beechdale as well. Me and Cliff were laughing like fucking idiots. He was nacking. We'd found a huge pile of gear for something fucking ridiculous like three hundred and fifty pounds a gram. Anyway, I'm fucking at it and Cliff's looking after everyone, but when we go back to the hotel he just says, 'Do you know what? I'm going to pass out.'

So we're there, and me and the other guy I'm sharing with have come back after partying for a couple more hours, and when we go back into the room, Cliff's still out cold. Obviously we're still pissed, so we're prodding him and shaking him, but he still ain't moving. He's out for the count. Nothing's waking this motherfucker up, so then we call Trenton in from another room. We go and get the shaving foam and cover him with that, then I've got a banana and put it in his mouth and I'm sticking my fingers up his nose and all sorts. We're photographing it all, but he's just snoring like this big fucking hairy hibernating bear.

We finally wake him up about twenty minutes later and show him the video. He leaps from his bed, covered in shaving foam, and all of a sudden this bear has turned into fucking Godzilla – 'You fucking bastards – *whaaaa!*' His arms are just flailing around, and we're all rolling around on the floor laughing.

I was talking to Kylie again a short while after his death, and she put me on speakerphone – it turned out that she and the whole family were in the chapel of rest, with Cliff's body, so I'm telling them all these stories and they're all laughing . . .

Once when we were in New Orleans, we were all partying and drinking Jack Daniel's and whatever else when we decided to go and eat. Cliff says, 'Yeah, man, I want to go to a proper spot, you know? I want soul food, I want some substance.' Now as a rule – especially on tour – Cliff listened more than he talked. He always used to put his head back, smile and go, 'Yeah, I hear ya, bro, I hear ya' – proper Birmingham. But this time it was him that was setting the agenda, and he found a soul food place, got the cars organised and we all got in the rides.

When we turned up at this place to eat, there were all these mommas – not one momma, loads of mommas – cooking up the food. Everyone was ordering at the table and we were just going at it. The food was disappearing in seconds and we were all checking, 'Is that my dish?' 'No, that's mine.' Cliff had just cleaned this plate when I said, 'Boy, he's just finished that, what was it?' And someone said, 'That'll be the pork.' And I was like, 'What? Cliff? You don't eat pork, do you?' He said, 'What? Was that pork? Oh my days!' He lifted his hat off his head like some Ol' Man River ting, and he's like, 'Oh God, man, Jesus, man, oh,' and we just burst into laughter, because Cliff would not eat pork.

So I'm telling Kylie this on the phone, and all the people there are laughing. Isn't that just what we need in times of sadness? Laughter, or music, to soothe us and turn everything around.

So when the BBC approached me to be part of a TV programme about classical music – 'OK, we're commissioning this show, and we want you to learn how to conduct' – I thought fucking Beethoven must be rolling in his grave: 'Not another fucking remix of a piece I've done so long ago! Not another fucking remix! Jesus, it's fucking awful!' Or would he go, 'That take on my music was played beautifully, I love that'?

I'm not fucking Beethoven, but I always remember hearing Matthias Vogt and his take on 'Inner City Life' with an ensemble. I don't want to confuse these: Roni Size did a mix and Peshay did a mix and 4 Hero . . . I love the boys, man, but it was all a little bit under par. It never quite . . . I don't know . . . It had angles, but it didn't quite work. I think the Baby Boy mix by Photek worked. But what was interesting was Gilles Peterson saying to me, 'You've got to hear this,' and playing me the version of 'Inner City Life' that Matthias Vogt had done. It was so amazing that I cried listening to that tune. Looking back over this book, I think I do that more than I realise. But don't you love that, when music makes you cry? Not just in a sad way, just because it's so beautiful. I asked Gilles if he had a number for this guy, then called him up in Germany. I was like, 'Oh my God, Matthias, it's absolutely unbelievable, the singing – who's the singer?' He was like, 'Oh, it's this woman, Jhelisa Anderson.' The name rang a vague bell, but nothing fully came through, so I said, 'Have you got a number for her?' And I called her up, and I said, 'Is this Jhelisa?' 'Yeah.' I said, 'I've just heard your version of "Inner City Life", and it's amazing,' and she was like, 'Goldie?' 'Yeah.'

She was, 'You don't remember me?' I'm like, 'Wwwwwhat do you mean?' Awkward smile . . . 'Haha.' She says, 'You don't remember me? I was going to do *Timeless* with you and then you vetted me for it, we spoke, and then I didn't get the gig because Diane got it.' I'm like, '*Aaaah*, I'll get my coat.'

It was awkward, but it was kind of beautiful at the same time, because of the soulful melancholy in her version of the song and her whole family's history in music, with her aunt (Vicki, who sang with James Brown as well as doing some great tunes of her own) and her cousin and her sister all being these great singers. But getting back to the point of doing the classical show, at first it was a bit like the *Celebrity Big Brother* thing, where people might ask, 'What the fuck are you doing that for?' And the answers to that question are: 'One, it's ridiculous money and, two, because maybe it's just a chance to get into that closed box and shake things around a bit, you know?'

Obviously the first thing most people think of in terms of the world of classical music is the perpetual exclusiveness of it. And for me it comes back again to one of my favourite quotes, which is from the architecture critic Joseph Rykwert in the film *Bombin'*, who said – of graffiti – 'The barbarians from within will take over and make a change,' but it applies just as much to classical music. It was just a chance to stand up and say, 'OK, so maybe I don't know what mezzo-forte means . . .' – well, I do now, because I was reminded by some cheeky twat in the front of the concert orchestra, who was like, 'He doesn't understand' – 'No, I don't understand, you fucking knob. If you just say to me, "Volume up" or "Volume down", I'll fucking get it.'

The whole thing with an orchestra is that if they don't fucking respect you, they won't fucking play for you – it's a bit like being a football manager in that sense. They probably won't tell you that, but that's definitely the word on the street, insofar as the concept of 'the street' is relevant to orchestras. So I had my clashes with certain people, like when I was trying to learn fucking *Carmina Burana* and one of the guys was taking the piss about me not understanding Italian, and I had to tell him, 'Look, mate, I don't know your fucking language. I'm just a kid from the 'hood that's up here on this podium trying to learn something about this fucking piece, so just be straight with me, man. And if you don't respect me, then, whatever . . .'

They kind of came on board after that – I think they realised it could've been a lot worse. The other people on the show were Sue Perkins, who I'd done *Celebrity Big Brother* with, Jon Snow the newsreader, the guy from Blur who owns the farm – I can never remember his name – and David Soul. I know what you're thinking – 'Don't give up on us, baby.' At the start we were all vetted by people who knew something about classical music and given mentors to help us. I was lucky to get Ivor Setterfield, who's a great guy – love him to death.

I think I drove him crazy at the start, though, to the point where he was actually banging his head against the wall, shouting, 'This is not going to happen!' He got the fact that I couldn't understand chords, because as someone who loves samples I'll have a chord in my head which is made up of all these different notes, but inside my fucking head I'll only hear it as one. The thing that had him shouting, '*Argh*. Fuck you! What is it you don't understand?' was the way I couldn't get my head around the way Beethoven's Fifth Symphony fitted together in terms of the time signatures. Then he had a brainwave: 'If I put it into numbers, will you understand it?' And, of course, because at some level music is maths, isn't it, that worked.

I've still got it somewhere, the whole of Beethoven's Fifth notated numerically: *duh duh duh duuuuh* 123 extended note *duh duh duh duuuuh* 123456, *duhduhduhduh duhduhduhdhuh*

    ALL THINGS REMEMBERED

duhduhduhduh 1234 1234 1234. Suddenly the whole thing made sense to me! And what opened it up for me even more was when I started to look into the story of Beethoven and it became clear – and I don't think this has ever been contested – that he was mixed race. His father was white and his mother was a Moor. And that made a lot of sense, not only in terms of the drawings and paintings of him with his wired hair and his flattened face but also the strand of B-boyism that I detected in his music.

A lot of people copied him, and what interested me was the way sometimes it almost felt like he didn't want other people to play his music. That famous Fifth Symphony in particular, it's almost like there are two records playing at the same time in 4/4, and someone knocks the left deck so the record jumps and then has to be put back. Again, I'm not comparing myself to Ludwig here (though that would be a good drum 'n' bass DJ name), but when I was making 'Terminator' I would cover the tune in a fucking hi-hat so it couldn't be sampled, the same way Jamaican sound-system DJs would take the labels off their records so no one could see what they were.

It's a total B-boy thing that if you take someone else's move, then you've got to better it. Like in breakdancing – if he spins on his back and then I spin on my back too, then I've got to go up on my fucking head as well. I've got to add something to make it more complicated, because you're constantly in competition. So you have to take the basic form – the base windmill, the headspin, the freeze – and then take it to another level, like the no-handed headspin, or spinning on the palm of one hand. So if you wanted to make it impossible for someone to copy you, you basically had to pre-empt that and anticipate all the extra flourishes that anyone else might think of bringing in. I think that's basically what Beethoven was doing. That intro to the Fifth is like the time signature from fucking hell: to most conductors who are seasoned, not a problem, but for me it took a bit of getting used to.

Now Technics turntables used to dominate the market share for DJs. Ironically, today they seem to want nothing to do with DJs. All they want to concentrate on is software, whereas their company's name was established by people in the urban community who made them very wealthy. The same way Moët champagne used to be the drink of choice in the 'hood – yeah, you drank your fair share at polo matches, but when the nineties came, and the noughties, I'm sure we made an impact on your sales figures, you know: 'We're also making money, we can celebrate.' But then all of a sudden the Moët people didn't want anything to do with the urban market . . . and it was the same with Technics.

'What the fuck has that got to do with Beethoven?' I can hear you asking. Well, the reason Technics turntables were so good was because as soon as you moved that vari-speed at the side of the fucking decks, it responded to you. Other decks came on the market, like Vestax, for example, and, boy, were they a fucking failure. And the reason they were a failure was because when you moved their vari-speed, there was such a latency that it didn't respond in the same way that Technics did. Well, the point about conducting is that you – the conductor – are the orchestra's vari-speed. You have the orchestra at your command, and you have to overcome that latency like a Technics turntable rather than a Vestax.

You've got to keep them on point. If you go too far forward, they start to accelerate too fast, but then once you realise they're playing too slow, it'll be too fucking late. You've got to be slightly ahead of them all the way, to the point that you know what's coming from the score; so now I'm looking at the score, I'm thinking, 'Oh, I can see all the highs at the top, I can see all the mids, and

I can see all the lows. Well, where are they? Well, my strings are here, just in front of me to the left, my wind is at the back with the brass, you know, to the right of me,' so you kind of know where they are, depending on the size of the orchestra, and you may even have a choir at the back of that. Ivor had done a lot of conducting choirs, so that was his speciality.

People were surprised it was possible to conduct without being able to formally read music, but even though I couldn't tell you what the exact notes were, I could follow the shapes, and I knew which instruments would play the highs and which would play the lows. So the score was a little bit like Braille that I could actually see – I think that's the best analogy I can come up with for it, although the whole dyslexia/synaesthesia thing probably comes into it somewhere as well.

The piece I was conducting in the show where you could really see me getting the hang of it was by Rachmaninoff. I felt so good I was almost taking the piss and going, 'Oh my God! I've got it!' Look, Ma, no hands! Except that wouldn't work in conducting, unless you were going to use your penis . . . which has just reminded me, I actually wrote a letter to Elgar, Rachmaninoff and Beethoven, thanking them for allowing me to be a witness on the inside of their music. After a while I really began to feel like I was aligning with their energies. Because when you're conducting and you're doing it right, the internalisation of the electronic artist just goes away, and you can feel the music channelling through your body – up out of your chest and down your arms to the tips of your fucking fingers.

All of a sudden you think, 'I'm now in control of this fucking piece! I'm in control of the orchestra, and I'm really engaging with them, so I don't feel like the end of my hand is this buffer between me and them; I've finally pushed this canvas away from me and I can experience the whole panoramic view. And I can feel the music like an electric current flowing through my body.'

You're controlling that room. You know where the fucking first strings and the violas are, you know where the brass is – nod to you guys. You can see the choir at the back there. You've got these guys here to the right. You're acknowledging everyone and you're pulling it out of them and keeping the speed right. Once you've gained the respect of the musicians, they kind of stop resisting and let go and allow you to manipulate them. Then you're all there in the séance together.

It was such an amazing experience that I didn't even mind not winning. Yeah, OK, a lot of people were a bit surprised when the public vote gave it to Sue Perkins – she hadn't even done *Bake Off* by then, so it was hardly like she was the people's fucking choice – but I'll be really honest with you: did I really want to be conducting arias in the park with that famous girl singer? Not really. So I think there was a good life lesson in that too, which is that sometimes it's actually better to come second, because underdogs have more fun.

G8. Fish and Chips without the Batter

There was a really beautiful period, maybe the two years before she died, when me and my mum spent some really fucking good time together. We'd found this feeling of empathy with each other that we'd never had before. It was while we were still living in Hertfordshire, before the move to Thailand, when she was ill. She'd come down to stay, and I'd sit with her sometimes. Koko would be at school and Mika might have gone shopping, and she'd sit there with her cup of tea and just burst into tears.

She'd say, 'I'm really sorry, son,' over and over, and I'd be like, 'Mum, just come on. Mum, you don't need to be. We're over it. Come on, man. I'm sorry too, you know, for being so angry with you' – because when we made the documentary *When Saturn Returnz* I was still really angry. I think that's why I caused myself so much pain – smashing my fucking left leg up, smashing my hand to pieces, always fighting and leading with my left . . . it was like the left side of me was where the pain wanted to live. Then she'd just go, 'There you go, bab, have a cup of tea. Tell you what, let's go shopping.'

I'd ask her what she wanted to eat, and she'd say, 'Och.' That's a Scottish thing, isn't it? 'Och, fish.' I'd say, 'I know what you want: you want fish and chips without the batter, right?' I'd always have to go to the fish and chip shop and get her fish without batter – which kind of defeats the object of British fish and chips, but Mom was gluten intolerant by that point.

I'd already been to Thailand a few times by then and I was looking into getting some land there. My mum would say, 'Och,

I'd love to go to Thailand. Bit too far, though.' So I think in her mind she knew she didn't have too much longer. But, bless her, she gave me a chunk of fucking money, man. I was selling the house by that point and she'd come down visiting with her little wheeled suitcase and my little nephew Javan, who's my brother's son. Javan was wicked – a lovely little kid. He'd always watch me painting and I'd get him involved – 'Oh, he loves his Uncle Goldie,' my mum would say. But his balls have dropped and he's a young man now, so he'd probably be a bit embarrassed to admit that these days.

Anyway, she'd come down to stay with this little suitcase and would seem really tired because of the cancer, but then I'd have to go out to do a DJ gig or something and I'd come back in the wee hours to find she'd woken up, come downstairs and completely fucking tidied the entire house. I'd have to tell Mika, 'We need to cancel the cleaners, because Mum's just given the place a complete overhaul.' She'd just go through every room, I suppose because that's what mums do. Then one time she said, 'I know you're short of a bit of money and I know you're going to go to Thailand, and I just want to make sure you're all right.' And she opened this fucking suitcase and started throwing all this money on the bed. I was like, 'Jesus Christ, Mum, what the fuck are you doing with that?' She said, 'Oh, I take it everywhere with me.' And I was telling her, 'Mum, you can't carry that kind of money around with you!' But she kept saying, 'Just take it, I don't need it any more, and I never gave you 'owt – take it.'

So I thought about it and I said to Mika, 'Mum's just trying to help me out here,' and I did take it – and the money went towards all the stuff we needed for the house in Thailand. I can definitely see the old dear in there now, in some of the rooms, especially when we're talking about her. Or when I'm thinking about

'Mother' – the piece I created for her with Diane Charlemagne. God rest Diane's soul, too. She's out there somewhere, singing to Ma and Kemi and Whitey and Cliff and all the wonderful people I've loved that I've lost . . .

SIDE H

H1. *The Journey Man* III – the Gospels According to Jon and James

The two big missing links with *The Journey Man* were James Davidson, the engineer from Ulterior Motive who I've already mentioned, and Jon Dixon, who plays keys with old-school Detroit techno legends Underground Resistance and has his own project called Timeline. I'd first met Jon at the Outlook Festival in Croatia, with Cornelius and Underground Resistance's Mad Mike, four years ago. The gig got rained off that year, and we were in a van going back to the airport when Mike said to me, 'You have to work with this guy.' So I was playing Jon some stuff I'd made, and he said, 'Wow, this is remarkable – it sounds like Pat Metheny.' And I said, 'You're not wrong.' And then we were off on this big riff about which of us was the bigger Metheny fan. I'm a competitive person but I've got to say that this one came out about even – I've never met anyone in an urban music environment before who loves Metheny as much as I do.

If that wasn't a massive omen, I don't know what would be, so I asked Jon to send me some demos, and about a year later, just as I was about to move to Thailand, he sent me these twelve pieces. Oh my God, they were unreal. One of them was a forty-eight-minute fucking piano improvisation – incredible stuff. And just the way that I am, I was listening to that piece over and over again, snatching bits out: take this intro, repeat that bit, bring that here, fold it around . . . I knew that was going to be 'Run, Run, Run', so I hacked an edit together with James, sent it to Jon, and said, 'This is the edit I want – can you replay this?' Jon was like, 'No, man, I can't. I can't replay this, man.'

He tried and it just didn't feel right. This was something that'd happened to me before – in fact, it crops up a lot. It happened with Noel Gallagher, when we were doing 'Temper Temper'. I wanted everything recorded, but Rob Playford forgot to press the button when he was warming up. So I said, 'Play that again,' and then Noel said, 'Play what again?' It's an age-old thing with me and working musicians.

I even reference this in the song 'Don't Give In', where I talk about 'My photograph of time'. Because that's what life is – a photograph of time. It's all about zooming into that photo. I'm here to photograph the magnificence of a player doing something I've always wanted to do and could never do, which is play a musical instrument. But try to photograph the magnificence of a player, man, and they're like flames in a fucking fire. They'll never play the same thing twice. Of course, if you record what they do and loop it, you can make sure they do. But the beauty of working with them is to go beyond the loop: that's what it's about, pushing against the parameters by not only looping their music but also extracting certain notes and moving them around.

I'd actually done this on *Timeless*, too, with a singer-songwriter and pianist called Robin Smith, who wrote a lot of Five Star's best stuff and will also always be a legend down under for helping to write the theme to *Home and Away*. He recorded an hour of piano improvisations, which I sang to him, and then I took the midi and inputted various synths and vintage keys and that became the bed of the twenty-one-minute track 'Timeless'. Thank you, dyslexia, for pushing me to make use of the sounds that no one wanted.

With *The Journey Man* it was James who did a lot of the sonic fetching and carrying. The original ideas for the album had been swimming around for maybe five years, then we did the drums a couple of years later, then the demos came in from Jon. In the meantime I'd moved to Thailand with Mika and Koko and it'd taken us maybe a year to settle in. Then the second year, which was 2016, I was speaking to James in detail, and he came over to make *The Journey Man* with me in April and May. It would not have been possible to do that without someone who's a phenomenal engineer and who, most important of all, doesn't question what I'm about to do.

Now Rob Playford, who I made *Timeless* with, was brilliant – way ahead of his time as an engineer, although he didn't make his own music, which I felt he should've done, but maybe he just didn't need to. He was also infamous, though, for the catchphrase, 'Nah, can't hear it.' I'm like, 'Well, you're not producing it. I'm fucking producing it and this is what I know's possible, this is what we can do, this is how it's going to be.' But sometimes people just don't want to engage with an idea because they think it's too much of a technical challenge – 'Nah, it's tough, it's not going to work.' 'Let's just try it. You don't know.'

I think of James Davidson as a complex AI – I can ask him whatever, and he's like, 'Yeah, cool, I can do anything you want.' However challenging something you might suggest is, he's always down with the idea. I mean no disrespect to any of the people I've worked with before when I say I've never met anyone like him, and he came into my life at exactly the right time – when I'd worn all the other engineers out. The thing about this game is, it's not a nine-to-five thing, it's really not; it's about setting yourself up, like for a fight. You train, you set yourself up, and then you go in – that's kind of what it is for me.

Having someone like James around was catnip to me – 'OK, James, first track on the album, "Prism", it's going to have a different time signature, it's going to have 3/3, then it's going to go back to 4/4, before it's even dropped, and then it'll drop into 3/3 on the break, and then it's going to drop back into 4/4.' 'Yeah, OK, let's just do this, cool.' 'OK, but we're going to try to do, like, dopplers and we're going to, you know, fuck around with analogue and we're going to fuck with digital.' 'Yeah, cool.' 'I've also got these modulars, man. I want to try these modulars.' 'Cool.'

James basically became family overnight. Blood, sweat and tears were not in short supply, and the greatest thing about working with him was that it never stopped. It must be those lithium battery cells he has. There were days when we were tired, but we couldn't wait to just get the sleep out of the way so we could go back in the studio and create more. There was never a hiccup. I tell a lie, there was one. The only hiccup on this entire project came when I was playing around with The Hangman break – which was one of the most used breaks in drum 'n' bass – and it just didn't work. It was almost as if I was going backwards, but sometimes you need to go backwards to go forwards. That's one of the most important things that I've learned – because that's how you discover jazz; that's how you discover a better music.

So I sat there with JD for eight weeks from April to May 2016, and we put together the sixteen tracks of the album. We replayed a lot of the demos to get them sounding really gnarly, then I built the tracks up like candy floss around them – we put them together from the inside out, section by section, like the middle of a fucking pyramid expanding to the outer casing.

My belief system is that this is how music should be – it's got to be built on a foundation that makes people stop in their tracks and go, 'Fuck!' I don't want to be DJing in a field at a festival looking out at a load of kids who seem a bit lost, as if they just don't really understand the music because they're too busy taking a fucking selfie, and that's what it's become. We need to teach kids to listen to music in another way – not just to listen to it, but to hear it – that's what the whole idea of *The Journey Man* is about: to help people along the road in the course of their own journey, on their route home, hopefully.

H2. *Classic Goldie*

After I'd done *Maestro*, the TV show about learning to conduct an orchestra, Roger Wright at the BBC asked me to come up with a classical composition – which became *Sine Tempore* – to be based on the theme of evolution, which was then going to be played at the Family Proms on a Saturday. I was like, 'Yeah, OK,' without necessarily thinking through the consequences of being filmed doing that. But I just watched the programme – *Classic Goldie* – for the first time in the eight years since it went out, and I actually felt really proud.

Not proud as in, 'Look at me wearing a gold shirt with a pair of fucking really dodgy shoes and dancing on *Strictly*.' That was all about the eighty grand in my bank account. Obviously that's not something to be proud of, really, it's slightly embarrassing, but it's still eighty grand, so let's not rock the fucking boat. That shirt was well dodgy, though. It's the hand pose: did you ever see that PR picture of me in *Strictly* where I've got that slight fucking eyebrow down, with the hands out like Paul Daniels – 'That's magic!'? Except it's not magic, it's fucking awful. Bloody hell. Note to self: monkey on a barrel organ, monkey on a barrel organ. Keep banging the fucking cymbals together.

Surveying the impact of classical music on my life before I started making TV shows about it, I suppose you'd have to go back to *Star Wars*, in 1977. The film came out, we all went to see it – for me, on a Saturday morning at the Miners' Club, somewhere in Willenhall – and then Christmas was coming. Christmas came, and you got the soundtrack to *Star Wars*, and you unwrapped the fucking album, but it wasn't the proper soundtrack to *Star Wars*, it was the soundtrack being played by a really bad orchestra, so it sounded totally fucked up. You just looked at it and smiled and thought, 'This is not the pair of shoes that I wanted.' It certainly didn't affect me the same way 'Mr Blue Sky' and Judie Tzuke did.

Beyond that, the person in my life who I associate most with classical music is probably Björk. Of course, Björk is a really powerful musical alchemist in her own right – she's created all this energy – but she also unleashed the full force of the Polish composer Henryk Górecki into my life. I'll never forget the house she had in Iceland, near the docks in Reykjavik. Looking out of the window, leading up to Christmas – and it was just covered with snow, with the sun and the moon in the same fucking skyline – and she was playing Górecki, you know, and that *Symphony of Sorrowful Songs* had such a profound effect on my life, and still to this day it's probably one of my favourite pieces of music.

Things between me and Björk obviously didn't end well after that fucking letter-bomber killed himself when he found out we'd got engaged and then all that shit went down at the airport, and I finished with her in the fucking sea in the middle of a storm. She was destroyed and I was burnt out, and all this other shit happened, and it was basically the end of the fucking world, so I'm like, 'Fuck this, I'm out of here.' We had actually gone to see a palm-reader not long before who said, 'It's not meant to be, there's two roads.' So that woman gets five stars on fucking Trip Advisor!

Anyway, apart from all the turmoil, one of the many beautiful memories Björk left me with was praying with her in the window of this flat with this beautiful piece of music in the background. And anyone who knew Górecki's work and then listened to 'Mother' could hear what a huge influence he was on me.

Maybe fifteen minutes into that piece, it's moving through the elements, and you hear the water, which represents being inside my mother's belly, and these shadows of a voice come in, which I guess are my spirit, and then the piece starts to stir with strings, the repetitive loops that are beginning, and all of a sudden those repetitive loops just flower, and I'm born. Then you experience the journey of a young child, and as the piece progresses onwards from the point of being born it kind of opens up to the strings, and then all of a sudden it becomes very dark and it gets pulled away, and the bottom falls out, and this abyss opens up below my feet, and I'm being torn from the mother. And, of course, that was me at the age of three, when I was abandoned and put into care. And from that point on I'm searching, lamenting for the loss of the mother.

Fast forward ten years or so, to me in the BBC having the early meetings about *Maestro*, and the guy I was talking to there handed me this DVD of a live version of *Symphony of Sorrowful Songs*, Górecki's Third Symphony, which had been recorded at Auschwitz. I can still feel the weight of it in the pocket of my Stüssy leather jacket as I went home. I put it in the player and watched it – I think it was a British singer, singing in Polish – and when the lyrics came up in subtitles, which obviously I'd never seen before, I could see that she was singing about the loss of her mother. That was a bit of a eureka moment for me – that this piece which I hadn't even realised at the time had influenced me so much actually had the same theme. It was one of the first times I remember hearing voices singing in a foreign language that actually spoke to me, where it wasn't like opera, which kind of bores me to tears. I guess that shows you the power of classical music to affect your subconscious.

It turned out that the guy from the BBC actually knew Górecki – he'd met him a few times, and even though Górecki was really ill at the time, he managed to get him to sign a score of *Sorrowful Songs* for me, which really meant a lot. I suppose all of this is also a roundabout way of saying that when I came to create that score for the BBC, it wasn't actually the first classical piece I'd written, but that didn't mean I didn't still have a lot to learn.

Maybe the best way of explaining the way I usually work with sound is to compare it to the Doppler effect – where an ambulance comes towards you, and as soon as it comes past you it kind of goes out of tune, because the motion of the vehicle kind of compresses the sound waves and then allows them to go slack. When I'm effecting the internalisation of sound that I have in a computer, that's kind of what I'm doing, and then the whole thing gets realised on playback.

Sometimes I'll be moving these blocks of sound around in a computer thinking, 'Now there's six sounds in there, but three of them are in reverse – there's a cowbell, a reversed string and one predominant note which I can twist around till it makes sense.' Of course, the great thing about doing that on a computer is that a snare can sound as loud as a kick drum, or a hi-hat, or a triangle, and any of them can sound as fucking heavy as a bass drum. What I found out the hard way doing the drum arrangements for *Sine Tempore* is that when you really have the fucking tom-toms and the kettle drum and the marimbas and all these other things in a room, they actually fucking obliterate each other. Ah: less is more – note to self.

Because we can compensate within computers: we can compensate with bringing down velocities and smoothing out the sound that's sticking out more than another sound, and side-chaining or identifying it as a solo. Whatever we need to do. It's coming out of two fucking speakers, for fuck's sake! It's not in a room full of all these players where the sound is being physically realised in front of you. So one thing I learned was that if I had all the volumes up to a naturalistic level on all of my arrangements, they would clash really badly in certain areas.

Another thing I learned – with the help of a really patient guy named Chris Mayo – was how to use a computer program called Sibelius. I don't know how that great Finnish composer would feel about having this particular piece of software named after him, but I guess we'll never know. Either way, it's got all the bells and whistles you could possibly need, and it came along just as I was thinking, 'I've got to reconfigure my internal operating system' – because that is how it feels with me sometimes, as if I've downloaded a certain amount of software but now the whole thing needs updating. I'm almost like a camera trying to focus in the dark: I don't realise what the lighting attributes of the situation are but I'm trying really hard to focus, zooming in, zooming out, then finally locking onto something.

What I'm really locking onto is that instead of having a set of strings within the block of sound that you sample, Sibelius allows you to create each individual cello or viola, layering them to create the chord itself so that the overall sound is nothing like your lush sample with the nice reverb. Aha! This is a different fucking beast, and because what I was trying to come up with was the sound of evolution, a different fucking beast was exactly what I was looking for.

I'd got to have the sound of the sea, and creatures coming out of the sea, so it'd got to be like insects crawling over rocks. Obviously Chris was going, 'Well, how do we do that? What sounds like insects?' And I was thinking, 'Well, a fucking tuba's not going to sound like a fucking insect, it will sound like a fucking mammal – it might be like a sea lion flapping his way onto the side of a rock, or a whale crashing into the fucking sea – but a fucking piccolo, or the plucking of a string, now that's going to sound more like a spider crawling across a rock, you know?'

So that took me back to basics, because I know my language within electronic music. All of the engineers that I've worked with know that when I say I want to do a fade-down, that means I want to ghost one of my earlier sounds: 'This is the loop that I want and this is the shape of the drum, and I'm going to sing it to you.' They understand that, because their mechanism is about capturing that break and that fucking edit. Now I don't know how I'm going to explain this in writing, but let's say I want to make a noise like 'eeeeeaaaaawwwwwaahhhhhhyyyyyip', so it's kind of a shearing-off sound with almost a triangle sound at the top but a low sound fading into it that could be the bowing of a string with a low cello, and a bass note which fades up onto it: '*Aah*, I get it.'

All I'm doing is changing my tools. It used to be paint cans, and now it's Sibelius. Or, to put it another way, imagine the sound I want is a China vase that has fallen off the shelf and smashed into twenty pieces. Now let's say the vase is painted really well, OK? And it's a picture of a dragon coming out of the sea into a forest. Are you following me? We push the vase off the shelf, the vase shatters into twenty pieces. So now the vase is all of these different pieces: it's a fucking jigsaw.

But I could pick up the piece that's the sea, and I can pick up the fire from the dragon's mouth, and I can pick up the part where the dragon is dragging himself into the fucking forest. Is the breakbeat going to be warm? Or is it going to be cold? That's going to depend on the effect that I wrap around it. I could package it up in a reverb with a really cool, steely delay. Or I could go for something warmer with little bit of fizz on it for effect. Either way, the great thing about Sibelius is that once I go outside of the fucking instrument's range, it indicates the notes in red, because that instrument cannot play that high. And that really made me think, 'Shit, I've got to adapt to this environment.'

So I have all of these instruments to suggest insects, and then these strings start to come in, and the original theme begins to adapt, and then the rhythm comes in and becomes syncopated because man has learned how to walk. And all the while I'm learning that anyone can make strings sound great on their own. But what's the fucking brass doing while they're playing that? Are they just sitting there on their hands? And then I'm realising that instead of me conducting this piece, Charles Hazlewood is going to be doing it at the Royal Albert Hall, so even as I'm putting my all into it, I kind of have to let it go . . . I guess that's what you call evolution in action.

H3. Mother VIP (Vocal Mix)

It was three years ago that my mother died, three days after my birthday – 22 September 2014. The last time I went to visit her in the hospital before she came home to die, she was in a really bad way with the cancer, but she was still fucking perky. She always was. I remember her moaning to me, 'Oh, they won't let me have my fags,' and blah-blah, just the way our mum was. I love her for it now.

The night my brother Stuart called me to tell me to get up to Wolverhampton because she was on her way out, it was ten o'clock when we actually got there. We picked Chance up on the way and took her up with us, and there Mum was in the front room in her fucking deathbed – classic black person's house, to have a 'living room' at the front no one ever used except for dying in. She'd picked this up from all the black men she'd had in her life – my dad, Pusey, and whoever else: you look around and all you see is crochet tings.

She still knew who I was when I walked in – 'All right, bab?' All the family were there – Melvin and fucking Jo Jo and all the fucking grandkids. It was mad. She was already drifting in and out, but then she started to get a lot worse, so we called the doctor again, but they were taking ages. I was angry about that at the time but in retrospect I can't really blame them – I blame the cuts for all that shit.

When the doctor finally arrived, they were preparing the morphine, and it felt like it was the end, but Mum still didn't want it. She didn't fucking want it. She was suffering so much she was screaming with the pain – well, not so much a scream, more

ALL THINGS REMEMBERED

an agonised, '*Aaagh.*' And her tongue was swelling and turning dark purple and . . . well, it was a long fucking night, let's just say that. We were all taking it in turns to sit with her, because the whole family was kind of exhausted. Then they gave her the morphine and she wasn't opening her eyes any more. I read the 23rd Psalm to her in front of all the family – you know, I'm not religious, but she had this Bible by her bed and I thought she'd want me to do that – but she was still there.

On one particular watch – at four in the morning or some shit like that – she opened her eyes and made as if to speak, but she couldn't. I held her hand and just hugged her, told her that I loved her and wanted her to be safe, and it was all going to be fine – 'Just let go, let go, Mum,' because she was going to be out of pain and she'd be in a better place, and all that stuff people want to hear, even though it's not necessarily true. I just hugged her and almost felt that heat from her body – the warmth of the mother which every child wants – and I squeezed her as much as I could without hurting her, and just felt her holding on and slipping away at the same time.

I went upstairs and cuddled Chance, because I was just in pieces, and then, at something like 10.30 in the morning, the breathing had finally gone and her tongue had gone black, and all the family were in the room and she just let out this one big burst and then she was gone. Or the nurse thought she was, but then she checked the machinery and she was still holding on – just fighting. And then, finally, two minutes later her mouth dropped open and the fucking life just fell out of her. So that was the end, but also the beginning of the next wave, where you're thinking, 'There'll be a break for a few years, but then it'll be your turn, with the kids by your bedside.' It was strange, but that was one of the first things I thought.

Death filled up the room, and I said, 'Look, just cover her

fucking face' – because she was lying there, with her mouth open. And then the fucking ambulance came, and the fucking women came, they said, 'You're not going to want to see this, you need to leave the room,' and we left the fucking room and they prepared her. Got her in the fucking bag. And they were patting the fucking bag, she's now like this lump – this woman that gave birth to you.

Everyone's bursting into tears and triggering each other, and as I've explained, I fucked off to New York and LA to do these gigs. I just had to get the fuck out of there. When I got to New York I spoke to Grooverider on the phone – I always speak to Ray – and also to Serena Gordon, who was kind of my mentor when it came to the Hoffman Process. I spoke to her for a long time, and she said, 'All of the strands are just coming back to you, and the elastic bands are all cut and coming back to her, and it's normal, it's natural, it's beautiful,' and that made me feel a lot better.

And then the thing after yoga happened. I was in that mental space you get into after yoga where you're just totally open and vulnerable. I was kind of in a daze, and I'd stepped into that hat shop – Lids, I think it was – then I stepped out and that guy from 'Bawston' bumped into me and I started a fight with him but then didn't fight back. I don't know why I did that – it was certainly the first time in adult life I'd done it, but I suppose maybe it was the child coming out, the kid who was bullied a lot and just took it. Maybe I just wanted to feel some pain.

I think some of us do that, whether it's actual, physical self-harm or getting someone else to do it for us. Maybe that's why some chicks turn into fucking hookers and want to get beaten up or whatever, I don't know. Maybe you want him to slap you up a bit, maybe you want to be a bitch for an hour, I don't know. Maybe you want to be a fighter, maybe you want to get in the ring, get beaten up, maybe you want to feel pain, I don't know. But for that moment, I felt that. I just held my hands down by my side, until he started laying some big ones, and then I put them up to protect my face, but still I never retaliated – just waited for him to run out of steam. And I was sitting there on the train afterwards with my head swelling up like I'd just eaten a bad fucking prawn, thinking, 'God, I feel better after that!' Weird. Primal.

Then I destroyed the place in LA by playing the VIP mix of 'Mother'. Then I came back to that chapel of rest in Wolverhampton, the Co-Op one, near Whitmore Reans, and on the way when Fritz was driving me up the M6 we had a really good fry-up – oh, it was a beautiful fucking breakfast! Still love a fry-up. You can take the kid out of the Midlands, but not the Midlands out of the kid, mate, I tell you.

Anyway, there we are at the chapel and I don't think I even had time to say I could kill a cuppa before the guy had got the kettle on and was making me one. I was kind of preparing myself, because much as no one else could ever understand why I would've made a sixty-minute track called 'Mother', this was kind of the day it was made for. I created this music as a way of reaching out to this woman who I'd had so much difficulty communicating with.

You know when they train monkeys that want food to twiddle particular knobs to get it? Well, you might think they're stupid, but maybe they're smarter than you think. Everyone thought I was mad to make that track at the time – and maybe I was a bit – but I also think I knew what I was doing.

Now I've got my headphones and my iPhone and my cup of tea. I want a cigarette, so I go and have one. Then I open the door and walk into the hallway, and there are maybe seven or eight doors. I think Mum's behind the third or fourth, and as I make my way along, there's just this slight tinge of a smell in the air – just this subdued chemical, clinical smell, from the embalming, with almost a stale tobacco note to it, which is probably from all the bereaved people they've had in there over the years who have been smoking heavily.

So I walk in, and there she is in her open casket, and as I step closer and see her hands placed on top of her chest, I lean forward and I can feel myself just fucking crying. I feel the tears rolling down my face and dropping on her marble corpse. I kiss her gently on the forehead and that feeling, of the stone-cold dead body, will never leave me, ever. This is not the same dead as being in bed with your mouth open a few days before, this is long gone, 'I've got my fucking coat.' I think I just said, 'Maggie, I miss you, Maggie, so much.' And then I sat there and I put the headphones on, as she wished, to listen to the song.

In *When Saturn Returnz* – which as I may have mentioned is a fucking disturbing documentary by anyone's standards, even mine; but, nonetheless, it's my life story and why I'm here – my mother said she wanted me to play it for her when she died. Doing this in the chapel of rest seemed like the most fitting thing I could do – because in a way this was the moment it was made for. And I did listen to it all the way through, although I think I paused it at forty-two minutes, not because it was so overwhelmingly long or anything, just because I wanted a fag and maybe another cup of tea. The guy goes, 'Refill?' I say, 'Yeah,' he makes me a second cup and then I go back in and listen to the rest of it.

Getting to the end of the track was a really, really beautiful moment, because it just allowed me to let go of her in a way that not even the funeral did. And that was that. I said my goodbyes and I came out of there, and I think she was in the chapel of rest one more night before we took her and buried her next to Pusey, her old husband. And I think that process – just the closure of it

– was the beginning of me wanting to reinvent my life. Because I was no longer a slave to the undertone of lamenting the early loss of her and the pain the relationship had brought us both. It was just a release, and that allowed me to move forward, and to move to Thailand. It felt like she'd let me go so I could go and live in Thailand. That was how it felt to me.

Just for the record, I should've been a better father.

In a way, I've lost two sons – one from a mental perspective and one from a physical – and I think, as a father, I failed on both counts. Nicholas was born out of an experience that was kind of a one-off, and there are some quite extreme issues with his mental health. I didn't know he was my son for years, because there was kind of an embargo by his mother, and I'm not really allowed to see him. I did meet him a couple of times, when he was brought down to London. He found it very difficult, and he has to have a lot of care in terms of his mental condition. I'm glad to say that he's in a more comfortable situation now than he has been, but that is quite a small shaft of light in a dark sky.

With Jamie, well, it's much harder for me to get out of the frame as far as what's gone wrong there is concerned. As is generally known, in 2010 Jamie was sentenced to twenty-one years in prison for a gang murder he committed two years earlier. I've admitted to him, 'I wasn't there for you, I wasn't a fucking dad as far as you were concerned.' And it must have been very shocking for him to have had this fucking strange guy turning up on the TV, or whatever, who's meant to be his dad, because he didn't grow up with me, and beyond that we never really had that father–son relationship.

Even with my third son, Daniel, I so much wanted to be a dad for him, but the whole thing went a little bit pear-shaped. The fact that he wanted to be a DJ and a promoter was difficult, because my footsteps have been hard for me to keep track of, let alone for anyone else to follow in. It was a big shadow for him to get out from under – you don't want people saying, 'That's Goldie's son,' you want it to be more, 'Oh yeah, that's Daniel, his dad's Goldie,' and I think maybe Daniel got a bit lost somewhere in the gap between those two things. But even with him there have been grounds for him thinking I have caused him trauma by not giving a fuck at certain points.

I wouldn't use the lack of an example in terms of a father figure in my own life, and the painful experiences of my childhood, as an excuse for any of this, because there are people who have had a worse start in life than me and yet still managed to turn that around. What I have tried to do is change how I behave, and also make a real apology to all three of them for the things I've not done for them.

My elder daughter, Chance, lived up to her name by giving me the opportunity to really come back at it. She's still suffered a lot of trauma because, you know, both of her parents are fucking nuts. And all the while she's been giving me this chance to have another go I have had an awareness that, as far as my track record at fatherhood is concerned, to adapt a line from *Snatch*: 'Choose your next action very carefully, because you're on very, very fucking thin ice, my son.'

I wish I'd have spent more time with her when she was young. And, of course, like in most of these kinds of broken situations, you separate, and you're fighting with the police on the doorstep, and you're fighting with the mum, and all that stuff's trauma for the girl, you know? I always feel saddened when I think about how much more I could've done, but I'm really trying to make up for it now.

I love the way Chance remembers things, and then I get into that space and remember it with her. Like being in the car on the way to the all-girls private school I sent her to, because I was getting paid then and it was like, 'Let's take her in the Bentley one day and the Ferrari the next,' just laying money down for the sake of it. Chance will say, 'Dad, I remember I was in the back of the car, you stopped and you had road rage and you pulled up in front of this guy and you got out and you were jumping up and down.' And I'm like, 'That's trauma, man!'

It wasn't all bad, though. Some of the songs we would listen to on those journeys – like Nathan Haines's 'Impossible Beauty' – will stay with me for ever. We'd sing that song all the way through together and then I would pull over and mime the saxophone part. Another time she asked me to put on 'Last Train Home' by Pat Metheny – that's when I knew she was a chip off the old block.

There were also times when me and her mother would get on, to a certain degree, but when it wasn't working out, it was a horror show. And as well as the arguments, Chance remembers me not settling down, and different women visiting me, and such like.

I had so much trauma myself as a kid, and then I kind of begat more of the same thing – I suppose because hate begets hate and love begets love – but now I'm trying to take responsibility over that and own it a bit. That's where Mika has really helped. Because obviously when I divorced Chance's mother and then remarried, that was a lot for Chance to cope with, and she didn't make it easy for us, but Mika was always like, 'This is what happens, you've got to help her, you've got to.' Mika never bit back; she's just made of a different gravy and understands all of these kinds of dynamics even though she's never had to carry this kind of baggage herself – whereas, of course, I came with three fake Louis Vuitton fucking suitcases packed full of all my bullshit, kilos and kilos of really bad emotions and me not being able to be a man, and all this other stuff from my past that had come through.

Chance had difficult teenage years, partly because she's very defensive – much like me. I had these moments which I can look back on now, but she's not at that stage yet, because she's still going through it. It's very difficult to tell a teenager, 'It's all going to pass, things will change,' because that world's so big, when you're in it. The whole private-school thing wasn't really working for her. She'd be laying into different birds – 'What do you mean? What are you going to do about it? OK, right, you want to make a scene, let's make a scene.' She's that kind of kid, just like her dad. Chance is never going to be a fucking dentist or an accountant, because the apple never falls far from the fucking tree; she's an artist, in some sort of way, and also an upstart.

She thought the world was against her – a touch of that victimitis I mentioned earlier – and sometimes maybe it was, and to some degree still is. But she's come through a lot of that now, to the extent where we can laugh about it a bit. Being in Thailand, with the different time zones, I'll sometimes be phoning her at five or six in the morning and catch her just going to bed. I'll be like, 'How are you, Chance?' And she'll say, 'Yeah, Dad. Good, man.' Then I'll say, 'I know that voice! That's the voice of really good weed, right?' And she'll start laughing. My daughter is proud to fall into the 'smokers' delight' category. And then I'll say something silly like, 'Yeah, but you know what it is, Chance? You know what I'm saying? Imagine if a fly gets on a plane in Africa and it comes back to England and gets off the plane, and he flies around with these other flies: does he speak the same fly language?' And then she'll laugh some more.

I hope Chance manages to get through her life without doing fucking copious amounts of blow like me, or drinking herself to death like her mum, God rest her. That would be a real achievement, because 2001–2005, man, when she was a little kid . . . fucking hell, I was really drinking heavily, and the cocaine was muting everything. If she can find a way through without that, she'll have done well. I'll be thinking, 'Thank fuck for that.' And

I'm already thinking that, because we have this amazing relationship now where I just want to spend more time with her. She's a gorgeous young lady, and I'm really proud of her.

Me and Mika having a baby together was a big challenge for Chance, with the whole sibling thing, and especially having to watch me be around for things happening in Koko's life in a way I wasn't when they happened in hers. I always beg her to forgive me for that, but I'm also hopeful that Koko can be the sister Chance always wanted.

Looking back I can see it would've been good for me to have tried a bit harder to stick things out with her mother, but it just wasn't working. And that's why I'm doubly blessed to find myself in the situation I'm in now with Mika and Koko in Thailand.

Koko is so like Chance was when she was young, it's amazing, and it's such a privilege to see life vicariously through her eyes. I take her to school on the motorbike, and the other day it began to rain, and she let out this really beautiful laugh – the kind that doesn't come from someone trying to make her laugh, just from her inner self, that place where she finds this joy, because the rain was hitting her face in a particular way. I asked her, 'What is it?' And Koko said, 'It's the rain, Papa, it's making me laugh so much.' And of course this triggered the emotions from when I was going through traumatic times when I was younger, and I'd be in the TV room of a children's home and it would begin to rain, and all the kids would have their eyes glued to the TV, and I would find myself slowly looking round at everyone in my field of vision without trying to move. Then I'd get up and, while their attention was elsewhere, I'd leave through the boot room, which was next to the TV room, and I'd go out through the back door and I'd stand in the rain and hold my head up to feel the rain on my face.

I still do that now. A lot of people just run for cover when it rains, but I love the way it bounces off my face and makes me

ALL THINGS REMEMBERED

feel like I'm more alive than ever. Unless I'm really late for yoga and I'm running and it's torrential, so the raindrops of magical laughter turn into ninja swords cutting into your face. Then it can become a feeling that's really strange and could even be quite abusive. So let's just keep the rain to a certain level, all right?

The fact is that when I'm taking Koko to school on that motorbike – through the backstreets and the paths of the beautiful Muslim village of Kamala – it's usually in lovely sunshine, with the light coming through the clouds over the mountain, and it's like I'm being allowed to remember, back past all the childhood trauma, which is something I've never been able to do before, but Koko is really helping me. It's just all about working out this fucking self-worth thing, man. I think we get so angry with people because we don't think we're fucking worthy, and then we just self-destruct. We're our own worst enemy. We can't let the fuck go. At least I couldn't.

If only I'd been able to fast forward to taking Koko to school on that motorbike. Because when you're being reminded about all of these beautiful things, the trauma seems to siphon itself away, or at least it kind of shifts so you can see through it like a fucking metallic gauze. And then Koko's there, going, 'I love Thailand, Papa,' and she's singing and she puts her bare feet up on the handlebars and it's like, 'Oh my God!'

Obviously this doesn't make it all right how fucked up things were for Jamie and Nicholas and Daniel (and, to a lesser extent, Chance). It almost makes it more sad in a way, knowing that now I can do better. But I just have to try to be happy that I can create memories for Koko that they – and I – never had, because being able to shape a young life in this way is such a beautiful privilege that even thinking about it makes me really tearful and excited about the future.

H5. 'If You Can't Say It, Spray It'

So I was living in this concrete jungle which was Heath Town, Wolverhampton. I was doing as much graffiti as I possibly could. I was doing so much graffiti that I'd run out of wall space – not just in the flat that I was living in, but on the whole estate. And for some reason the police couldn't catch me. It became crazy, it became whatever it was. And then, all of a sudden, thanks to *Bombin'*, I was in New York meeting my heroes – physically living the dream.

There's an interview with me on YouTube from that time in New York, wearing a fur coat, with a drink in my hand, but not pissed, just relaxed in myself – full of beans, full of balls like steel, full of everything, every bit of sperm is kicking hard. I'm just drenched in ego, spunky as fuck, totally fucking ruling. My accent's all over the place because I'm talking about these New York graffiti guys and so there's a little bit of them in there, a little bit of West Midlands hanging on for dear life, and even a little bit of Ireland out of nowhere 'cos that's where the inter-viewer came from.

I adapt. That's how I was and still am now – I adapt. I guess it's partly a children's-home thing. When you've got all those lockers with all that different music in it you've got to find a way to fit in, and you've got to find a way to stand out. So when suddenly you're on Staten Island doing this graffiti piece and the artist who you've looked up to from afar says, 'You ready for this, man, you fucking English boy?' you've got to be able to say, 'Let's make this happen,' straight off the bat. I remember he laughed. It was the same when I was in Miami, in the flea

markets, people would speak to me in Spanish, which obviously I don't understand, but I would still interact with them: 'Yo . . .' I'll play, I'm street, I get it.

When I got back to Wolverhampton, once *Bombin'* had come out, and also because of the big graffiti events we'd done locally (like the one where Brim Fuentes came up to Birmingham library), I'd have kids coming up to Heath Town on little pilgrimages. Not like the organised ones you see now around Shoreditch – official tours of the graffiti museum – just individuals who were into it finding their way up to Heath Town from Birmingham, Coventry, Leamington Spa to look at the graffiti. It was nice to have given people a good reason to go to the place I lived in, because there hadn't been many tourists before. Sometimes these kids would catch me on the estate and I'd bring them back to the flat and school them out and tell them stories about New York. I guess there was a bit of a Pied Piper vibe going on and, alongside the roller-hockey and the breakdancing, it was an early taste of being a bit of a celebrity on the underground, which I liked.

Another thing that had happened in the course of *Bombin'*

was that I'd met Robert Del Naja. I was quite competitive with some of the other UK graffiti writers – especially Mode 2 and some of the London guys – but I never saw Delje as a rival, always as an ally, especially once he'd given me the tape with Miles Davis's *Decoy* on it, which fucking blew my mind. I think I met him at Bristol carnival first, for *Bombin'*, and the big graffiti show at the Arnolfini gallery, and then we did a video for the band Westworld up in London, in Hammersmith somewhere, where we were painting this Mini on the set. I think that was the first time I did speed – I didn't realise it would keep me awake for three days.

I was a bit of a bad lad in those days. I used to go down to Bristol in my gold three-litre Rover – no tax, no insurance, sawn-off shotgun in the boot, which I'd then carry round in my coat like I was in the fucking *Sweeney* or something. Even how we got that car showed what wannabe gangsters we were. I saw an ad in the paper for this car for sale for £500 down in Leicester. Five or six of us went down – me, my brother Melvin, a couple of other brothers – and we basically strong-armed this kid on an estate. I think we gave him £275 for it. It's not my proudest moment, but at least we didn't leave him completely empty-handed.

Anyway, we took this car back to Wolverhampton and I used to drive it around like a madman – big boombox on the back shelf, because the stereos back then weren't cutting it. The batteries that thing used to get through, it was unbelievable – the big heavy ones, too. I used to commission kids to nick them for me in return for a couple of spliffs of weed and, of course, the privilege of finding me batteries. I was a proper little Fagin on the estate. At that time I was living next door to a gambling house in a block called Hawthorn House, so because my door was always open, people often used to walk into my flat thinking they were gonna win some money.

I'd often end up bombing down the M5 to Bristol for sound-system house parties in St Paul's. It was a mental time – as well as Delje, I met Mushroom, Tricky, everyone, all of what would become Massive Attack, who were then mostly in The Wild Bunch. Milo was the main man, though.

It was almost as if hip-hop culture had dropped like a glass in England, and the glass had shattered into different pieces. Manchester had the breaking, Bristol had the parties, London had the breaking and a few of the parties, Birmingham and London had the graffiti.

When I was first at the Dug Out club in Bristol with The Wild Bunch, I was just there as a punter – it was the next step on from the Half Moon Club, really. To me, when I first met them, the Bristol people were the absolute bollocks. They were the start of me realising that all those breaks on those mixtapes I had actually came from somewhere. They brought in that crate-digging aspect and opened the way for me to go back to the source, which was what rare groove was all about. I didn't even know what that was till I saw The Wild Bunch and heard Nellee Hooper playing songs like Maceo and the Macks' 'Cross the Track'.

That was when I started to realise that these breaks were frozen in time. There's a kind of concertina effect where all these ripples from the past come through, but into your present. Another record which made a huge impression on me was 'If You Don't Give Me What I Want (I Gotta Get It Some Other Place)' by Vicki Anderson (Jhelisa Anderson's aunt) – the piano on that record haunted me for years. It was almost like it politically motivated me, but not in a political cause, more in terms of being drawn to these chicks who were getting a hard time from the guys that were getting all the kudos for the music. It was almost like, 'Yeah! Right on!' – even though maybe that's a bit ironic, given that I wasn't treating the women in my own life very well at the time. But I think it was an early awakening for me in terms of how the feminine side of music really works: hang on a minute, the real soul of the music is not about the guys.

I guess the aggression would kind of get pent up by the oppression of society, because someone's got to get food in the kitchen, but once it's there, then someone's got to cook it. I always felt that whenever there was an argument in a children's home, or with foster-parents, the kitchen was the place I remembered going to make it all right: that was where the love came from. And it was the same with the music. As I was trying to work out what it was about these tunes that drew me to them, I started going to Salvations, which wasn't religious, but a club that played rare groove, and I guess there was a big spiritual element in a lot of that music.

Once people like Public Enemy started to come through I could really feel that music – but at the same time also all the original music that the samples had come from. That was like stepping through the cartoon to find Eldorado for me – you go through the waterfall and you're in another world of the original music with the breaks in it. And it's not just a music of black origin thing either, because you're thinking, 'That's why De La Soul are so soulful, because they're borrowing from Hall & Oates!' – who are obviously borrowing from black music in their turn, so it all becomes this big circle. Like if you think about 'One More Night' by Can, could you honestly try to tell me that is not a soulful record, even though it's made by a bunch of far-out German guys and their Japanese mate in a fucking studio taking LSD?

As usual, it was all about lamenting the loss of the mother for me – locating the soul in music. That's probably why I have so many female vocalists onstage with me and so few male ones if you see me play live now. It's also maybe why I wasn't so drawn

ALL THINGS REMEMBERED

to the early stirrings of UK hip-hop that were coming through at the time. You might think that would've been a logical way for me to go when I came back from New York full of the excitement of the Bronx, but in a way I think that was what stopped me doing it.

Don't get me wrong, I liked Rodney P and Bionic from the London Posse, and for me Silver Bullet was way ahead among UK rappers. Cookie Crew going out to America was also a big deal, but I didn't feel any desire to emulate what any of these people were doing. I almost felt – as strange as this might seem given that I was living in Heath Town doing graffiti at the time – that the social backdrop we had wasn't depleted enough for the music to quite sit right. Like it's time hadn't come yet – Wolverhampton could be bleak, but it wasn't the Bronx. When I went there and saw what they were singing about I just thought, 'Fuck, this is not a game, they're actually really singing about it.'

It was a similar thing a few years later for me when drum 'n' bass started. Because I'd done the reggae thing in the eighties, when I was wearing a sheepskin and growing dreadlocks and the power of the bass bins at the Half Moon was making me physically sick, I didn't feel the need to have jungle MCs on the tracks I was doing. It was a bit 'been there, done that' for me, and I think that's where some of that divide came from.

New York was always the Mecca, and I felt Britain needed music of its own. I think the industry wanted Americanism, that's fair to say. And I think the buildings and the guns and knives that the US rappers were singing about were a glamorous fascination which we hadn't quite experienced yet, which was why the language never really stuck. That's also why I was so excited when the rave scene started happening – because a load of people gathering in a field essentially saying, 'We're not anything, our music is faceless,' and being berated by the Thatcherites, that felt like more of a homegrown thing to me.

I guess drum 'n' bass, and then maybe grime, ended up being the fulfilment of what homegrown UK hip-hop would sound like. In my opinion French rap was way ahead of ours in the eighties and early nineties. I think maybe the social conditions they had on their HLM estates were maybe more in line with the projects of New York, and the fact that they had to rap in their own language made it easier for them not to copy the Americans. There was certainly speed in their dialect: you only have to watch *La Haine* to see that.

I remember when the south London graffiti writer Mode 2 moved to France it felt like he was ahead of his time. Although there was a certain amount of animosity between us – hip-hop kind of bred that, and we did feel that a bit with the graffiti writers from London, though I don't know if it was them getting on our backs or vice versa – he taught me a lot about graffiti, because he was really good at characters. In fact, I think he's been one of the greatest graffiti writers of all time. We got on fine later on – and still do now. He sent me a great book of his with the inscription, 'From bitter rivals to close friendship,' and I even asked him to paint a *Saturnz Return* billboard for me.

For me, graffiti was always – and still is – the movement within hip-hop culture that I've felt a part of the most. That's why I'll always feel so close to people like 3D and Mode 2, because we speak with the same aerosol tongue. I guess the concept of the hieroglyphics – physical representations of a language that I could understand even if some other people couldn't – was a big deal to me, and not least from a dyslexic perspective. The vibrancy of the word 'love' resides in the colours it's filled with, more than the word itself – I think that's what I'm trying to say. It couldn't be spoken about, but it could be shown.

H6. Doc Scott

So I'm in Sardinia, with Scotty, who has always been my left-hand man, and is definitely one of the major characters in the history of drum 'n' bass. He was there right at the beginning and he's still at the top now, so there's no one better to talk to about the gentrification of the genre.

You'll have guessed that we've reached the second point where this book turns into a dialogue. It's not exactly like that Inside the Actor's Studio *TV programme they used to have on Sky, more like two people sitting on a hill overlooking that. Because we had this conversation in late 2016, right when the whole storm about the London super-club Fabric getting closed down was breaking, that was obviously the starting point (I know that story's moved on since then, but what follows is true to how we felt about it all at the time).*

Goldie: Trying to put this whole Fabric thing in perspective, I guess we do have to acknowledge that on one level, in historical terms, clubs closing down is inevitable. If you think about the Haçienda in Manchester, there wasn't anything bigger than that when it was happening, but all of a sudden it's closed and someone's probably going to get a bit of the flooring as a souvenir. I've actually got part of the bar from The End – Mr C from The Shamen's place. When that closed down I got this really heavy piece of wood – it's like a piece of art. So I wonder what sort of tap someone's going to have from Fabric?

Scott: They'll probably turn the booth into a bunk bed.

Goldie: The difference is that with The End, at least they gave that place a proper ending – I suppose it had to have one, given the name. They stretched out it over three days. I remember Fabio playing the last set in there, and he played my song 'Terminator' as the final tune. I'll never forget that. The thing that came to mind with Fabric was that it was like a cancer patient, where it's good to be able to respectfully say goodbye before they wither away and die. People got confused about me saying, when it happened, that I might as well melt down my MBE. I wasn't saying I was actually going to do that, just trying to capture how confused I was about the way the whole thing went down.

'Goldie threatens to melt his MBE down.' Guys, I'm making a very fucking valid point, for the record. Would the council like me, Trevor Nelson, Omar, Jazzie B, Norman Jay – you know, all these people – to melt our MBEs and make silver spoons to stir their rather sweet coffee so they can celebrate crushing culture and all it stands for, after people have spent years on this journey through music? What I'm saying is: why would we ever do that? It's a rhetorical device to show how fucking stupid this situation is. But then you get people saying, 'Oh, how insulting. It's so disrespectful that you would want to melt down something that the country's given you.' That's the answer to the conundrum, you idiot! I'm saying that closing one of the most culturally significant clubs in the country is just as destructive and pointless as melting a medal down would be. The answer is, 'Exactly: this is just as bad that you've closed one of the most cultural clubs in the country.'

Because in terms of the young people who are coming through, when you close a place like Fabric down, it's like a kid who wants to be a runner, and they see that Usain Bolt has won lots of of medals and is the best in the world at 100 metres, but then in

ALL THINGS REMEMBERED

Jamaica they've closed all the athletics clubs, so it's like, 'What do I do, Dad, if I want to be a runner?'

Scott: Exactly. Because I was quite vocal about the closure of Fabric when it happened I've had a lot of people coming back to me saying, 'Oh well, it's just a club. There'll be another one, and you can do drum 'n' bass nights somewhere else.' But for me it's not just a club, it's what Fabric symbolises. It's been a symbol of UK underground dance music for the last fifteen-plus years, and the reason I'll always have a special place in my heart for Fabric is that they never turned their back on drum 'n' bass, even when other clubs did. Room 2 was always a drum 'n' bass night on a Friday, even when everywhere else was turning their nose up.

Goldie: I saw Paul Pendulum tweet a thing yesterday saying, 'I can go away and know Fabric's going to be there, but if I go away and it's not . . .' Even if you're not there, it's that safety belt. But it's not even really about us, it's about the next generation.

Scott: My son Noah is thirteen years old, and I'm forty-five now, so he'll turn eighteen when I'm fifty. At that point he can legally come out with me to a gig or whatever, and I'm not just thinking in terms of Noah here but kids in general. Where are they going to be able to go out to listen to music to learn what we learned, to become the people that we became, whether that be DJs or producers, or even just punters who are knowledgeable, who can go out and know what a good DJ is, what a good drum 'n' bass set is? If you keep taking away these places, where are they going to learn their stuff? For me, this is already happening. With some of the music I've been sent over the last five years, I can hear the fact that the people producing it have maybe never been out to a real club or heard a real DJ. Because it's all—

Goldie: Internet-based! And if it is a club, it's not the grimy one. Say it might even be festival-based, that ain't the place to go out and cut your teeth musically, is it, really?

Scott: I don't think so. A lot of these kids, they only listen to drum 'n' bass, and they don't listen to anything else, whereas we grew up listening to hip-hop, electro, jazz, film soundtracks, whatever, so you had this diverse palette to pull from, and then we started to make music ourselves. Ten years from now, is the DJ just going to go into their booth at home and play, and then everyone's going to sit at home with a PlayStation 4 . . . or 7 . . . 12 and put a fucking virtual reality headset on? If that's where we're heading, man, I'm definitely quitting, because that's horrible, that's a horrible, horrible vision.

Goldie: A virtual nightclub – what a load of bollocks. If there's anyone out there who hasn't seen it, check out that video of David Bowie and fucking Mick Jagger doing 'Dancing in the Street' with the sound taken out. That's what silent discos look like to me. It's fucking hilarious, it's so stupid. But I think the gentrification of clubland is taking everyone that way. A lot of the DJs now are like, 'Quick, two minutes in, if I don't play something now . . . they're not moving . . . shit, panic,' but I don't think being a great DJ is just about making people jump up and down.

Scott: Not all the time. When I play, I deliberately take things down, because I like peaks and troughs, do you know what I mean? You get certain tracks and you know, 'That's a peak tune,' and I get sent other things and I know, 'That's a bridge tune, that's a trough tune.'

Goldie: They're kind of unravelling something that I think can't be put back. Not just in terms of all the people, the money and the jobs that are involved in clubs in general – from the DJ to the guy doing security – but also through the broader impact these places have on society at large. If I had a pound for everyone I bump into in some really fucking bespoke media building who comes up to me and says, 'I went to Blue Note, man.' The rest of the creative industries are full of people who cut their teeth in underground nightclubs, and because of the breadth of the music they heard in those environments, it actually opened their minds up to the arts in general. So on the one hand you've got all these people like Pete Tong and Norman Jay who've changed the system from the inside and become really important figures, all out of club culture; then on the other you've got some guy in a local council who's probably quite miserable and never really went out at night, and he gets to shut them down.

Scott: When I saw the question in the inquiry where they tried to imply that the deaths of the two kids who died from drugs after going to the club were beats-per-minute related, that's when I knew that Fabric was doomed. The whole thing became a farce, more like something out of *This Is Spinal Tap* than an actual legal process – it's like, 'Slow the music down so that the kids might live . . .'

Goldie: What are we supposed to do, ring up our mates in Brazil and say, 'Can you please stop salsa music? Because it goes at 175bpm, and the whole population of South America is in danger. Everyone at the Carnival in Rio could die from a heart attack because the music's too fast.' There are plenty of other genres this applies to, by the way – parts of Berlin and the whole of the gabba scene should definitely all be dead by now.

Talk about sonic terrorism! The irony is that the real sonic terrorism is criminalising the environments which people go into to hear music.

Scott: It would make so much more sense to do what they do in Holland, which is to accept the fact that a certain percentage of young people are going to experiment with drugs – not necessarily because they go to a club and dance to the music and those things are particularly bound up together, but if they go to a classic car festival or just stay in and watch a music video. It's going to happen whatever environment young people are in. So they have these places where people can test whatever drug it's meant to be so they can see what's actually in it, whether it's been adulterated. I do actually think testing might be the answer. They tried the 'Just Say No' thing when I was ten years old with Zammo in *Grange Hill*.

Goldie: Crazy – Zammo, brilliant, 'Just Say No'.

Scott: But that was in the eighties, man, the age of Reagan and Thatcher. It's 2016. Just say no is not, is not—

Goldie: It's not going to work. And also you don't know what's going on in that particular person's situation. Let's think about the backstory of them as human beings, and what misery they might've gone through in their own lives to bring them to this point. After being in various stages of drug addiction myself for not far off thirty-five years, I know how many times I've woken up surrounded by the paraphernalia of alcohol, pills, powder and everything, thinking, 'Jesus Christ! I'm lucky to be alive.' Now let's say I'd not been so lucky, but I'd somehow been overseeing that situation as a third party, wouldn't I be the one thinking,

ALL THINGS REMEMBERED

'Fucking hell, you silly cunt, think about the shit some people have gone through and you were a lucky bastard to even be
alive'? At that point, there's no one I can blame my own death
on other than myself. You can't just go, 'Everyone at the funeral,
let's just blame Doc Scott for playing the music at 170bpm,
because Doc killed him.' It's fucking ridiculous . . .

Scott: Every loss of life is beyond tragic, it really, really is, but
we've seen the news. We've seen the articles that came out after
this decision to close Fabric – the whole Smithfield thing, the
involvement of the museum, the Lenor report. There are at least
two other stories here: one is a story of ulterior motives as to why
they want the land Fabric is on; and the other is about using the
drug thing as the reason to close the place.

Goldie: Some people have said to me, 'But don't you think
Fabric failed to take enough measures to stop people taking
drugs on the premises?' At that point I'm like, 'Man, you can get
a dog to stand on its hind legs, but doing a back-flip is another
thing, and what you're basically asking them to do is train a dog
to DJ. You're asking a fucking dog to go fucking back to back
with fucking Grooverider.' Because the security in that place
bent over backwards to keep things legal. Or, to be more pre-
cise, they'd have you bending over backwards, so they could
stick their fingers up your arse and fist-fuck you to find an E.

Scott: Absolutely, man. I read some of the quotes from the
undercover police officers who were supposedly in Fabric, and
it wasn't the place I fucking knew, man. That club had the most
stringent security I've ever come across in twenty-five years-
plus of DJing.

Goldie: There were some places in the eighties where security would drag out anyone they caught selling drugs because they had their own people doing it . . .

Scott: That was rife back in the day. There was one place where if they caught people selling drugs in there, you were given the choice: you were chucked out and they took your stuff off you, or they broke your hand with a hammer. I saw it! I was waiting to get paid once, and some poor guy's in there, they got a big mallet out and smashed his fucking hand up. At least we've moved on from there . . .

Goldie: In terms of shenanigans that have gone on in clubs, Fabric was not even on the same planet of debauchery as fucking Studio 54; it was nothing like the Dungeon in south London. I know clubs that were beyond hedonist, man. Eclipse, let's talk about hedonism. To be fair, Fabric's a lamb compared to the rest of fucking UK clubbing. An absolute lamb, and if they're going to make this the yardstick that all the others have to measure up to, then every club in the country is going to fail. So OK, where's next after Fabric? Are they going to go after Fire next? And then they're going to go after Ministry, till you're literally left with nothing in London? London is like a fucking beacon around the world. We go around the world, right – we go to New Zealand, Australia, Japan, America – and they're all looking to London to see what the next thing is and what the next sound is and where's drum 'n' bass going, what's the next turn. Look at the way grime's being exported now. We are the ones that do that. You know, like with rap in the nineties – how are you going to sell a hip-hop act in America? First send them to England, then to Europe, see if you can break them there, before it comes home on the rebound. People forget that in the industry, that's how they broke American acts.

Scott: Look at Public Enemy – *It Takes a Nation of Millions . . .*
– all those samples were from that gig they did at the—

Goldie: Hammersmith Odeon.

Scott: London makes a noise. Do you know what I mean? Fuck, man, are you going to take those venues away so that when the next Public Enemy comes along, when they want to come and play in the UK, there's no fucking places for them to play? So we're just left with . . . what? Fucking YouTube? I do believe that creative souls will always find . . . you know, if it's within you, you will dig out the music; you will find dBridge, you'll find the new release on Metalheadz that's buried down there, the one that kind of skims under the surface, not the big, shiny ones. But you still need to give people the opportunity, so they have the choice.

Goldie: It's like someone hears some track on YouTube and they think that's all that drum 'n' bass is, because it's in the chart and it peaked at 24, even though it's actually shit. That music has as much class as a man telling a woman, 'I want to make love to your face.' It's mutton dressed as lamb.

Scott: You always need something to compare something to. If you don't have anything to compare . . . if all you're getting fed is stuff that you can get off the shelf at Tesco's, and you've got nothing to compare it to, then you're going to think that food is great.

Goldie: You know there's Iceland as well, we've got Iceland? Iceland's second choice, let's face it, do you know what I mean? But we shop at Waitrose: you know that?!

Scott: Of course we do.

Goldie: It's also how it's presented, as well.

Scott: Of course it is, man. It's like a chef. You take the fucking food, you can get the best steak in the world, you cook it wrong, you're going to give people food poisoning, do you know what I mean?

Goldie: Great analogy, man . . . Long time, Scotty, fucking hell.

Scott: I know.

Goldie: Sardinia, two thousand fucking sixteen, me and Scotty.

Scott: Peace, we out.

I'm coming towards the end of the fifty-second year of my life now, but when I sit outside on the balcony of my house in Thailand listening to Erik Satie's *Gymnopédie No. 1* – you'll recognise it because it's the music to a Cadbury's chocolate commercial – I get transformed into the most peaceful kid. It's like I'm twelve, but the good twelve, when you've been through your pre-puberty Stalin phase of planning insect atrocities with Paul Gough, but haven't quite started masturbating yet.

I appreciate the fact that my musical time machine is still working for me – it's not rusted up as I've grown older. Another happy knack I don't seem to have lost is the one I've always had for bringing really good mentors into my life. My friend James – a teacher from Boston who, with his wife Christine, runs the school my daughter Koko goes to – is one of those beautiful people who manage to calm the areas of my mind that I need to keep still.

James is only forty-seven but he's already such a reluctant shaman that he reminds me a little bit of Alec Guinness playing Obi-Wan Kenobi – to the extent that I wouldn't be surprised to see the Sand People approaching when he comes into view. We have this ritual together which we call 'sea-chi', where we get up at five o'clock, swim around in the sea and have deep phil-osophical conversations for a while, then go to the school, open up the gates and do chi kung in the same yard Koko will play in later in the day. James must get déjà vu sometimes, because she really looks like me – the living stamp, as they say in Jamaica.

Chi kung is a kind of moving meditation which is very

conducive to abstract thought. I'd recommend it to anyone. One of the ideas James and I came up with during sea-chi was that 'life is a singular sequence of consecutive miracles set within infinite moments over billions of years'. We were pretty happy with that one.

The other thing James and I do together is play backgammon. I don't have the sleight of hand and quickness of fingers that the Turks have, but I'm getting better. And one of the things I really love about the game – maybe because of some of the dyslexic qualities my brain has that mean it won't allow itself to be regulated in that way – is that it's the opposite of chess. Chess is all about hierarchy – the kings and queens and the rooks and the pawns and the manipulation of society and, 'We, the royal ones, should deal with this or that or there will be anarchy.'

Backgammon, on the other hand, is just pieces – black and white . . . and I don't see this as a racial parallel, they could just as easily be tan and dark tan. The important thing is that they all have the same value, so the game is more democratic – like the

ALL THINGS REMEMBERED

rave scene as opposed to the rock scene. There's no sense of one being worth more than the other, and the only thing that decides their destiny is the dice.

Yesterday I got an ass-whupping – twenty-five points to three or something ridiculous – but the day before that I completely smashed James up. It doesn't matter who you are – a homeless guy or a millionaire – the dice will be against you one day, but then the next you'll throw three doubles in a row. That's what my life's been like, too. Sometimes the universe gives you doubles – I've had more than my share of those – but sometimes it fucks you up the arse. There's no point in wondering why that happens or who decides which way the dice fall on a case-by-case basis; you've just got to let that thing go.

At this stage in my life I feel that's the answer to more and more of the questions I ask myself. If I'd kept everything I ever possessed, my house would collapse. You'd never get all those flash cars and all of that designer sportswear in there, for a start. There'd be no room for them, and no room to be free.

@ ITS THOSE MOMENTS IN MY LIFE THAT
I WAKE IN THE DEAD OF NIGHT, THAT
YOU REALISE WHAT TRULY MAKES YOU HAPPY
HAVING THOSE YOU LOVE CLOSE TO YOU, AND
BEING THANKFUL FOR WHAT YOU HAVE AND
KNOWING THAT THIS IS YOUR HEAVEN THE UTOPIA
YOU HAVE CREATED TOGETHER. SO I GUESS THE
HELL OF IT ALL, IS NOT BEING ABLE TO REMEMBER
ANY OF IT WHEN WERE GONE BUT KNOWING
YOU HAVE LIVED AND CREATED EVERYTHING YOU
EVER DREAMED OF IN YOUR PURSUIT TOWARD
HAPPINESS. LISTEN TO THE SOUND OF YOUR SOUL
AND IT WILL MAKE YOUR HEART SING. ALWAYS
REMEMBER ... THAT A TRUTHFUL IDEA WILL LAST
IN THE HONESTY OF TIME.

TATs HEADZ.
W·D

LOVE AND LIGHT ALWAYS

Ben Thompson thanks Lee Brackstone and Sav Remzi, first for giving me the job and then for helping us get on with it; Goldie for being a delight to work with; the House of St Barnabas for giving us a great place to meet; Adam Brecher for lending me the Henry Chalfant book; Liz Dexter for speedy and meticulous transcription; Nicola Barker for remix concept, titular nod and editorial precision as always; Karl Nielson and Mika Wassenaar for being totally on it; Ian Preece, Dave Watkins and Ian Bahrami for meticulous stewardship on the home straight; and Kelly-Lee Alexander, Leila Arab, Will Ashon, Maya Biltoo, Russell Davies, Nicholas Detnon, Dizzee Rascal, Vicki Duffey, Susanne Freytag, Richard King, Simon Petty, Jon Savage, Wesley Stace, Matt Thorne and Nicole de Zoysa for helpful conversations and correspondences.